EXPLORING
THE
HIDDEN
HIMALAYA

EXPLORING
THE
HIDDEN
HIMALAYA

SOLI MEHTA
and
HARISH KAPADIA

THE HIMALAYAN CLUB

published for
THE HIMALAYAN CLUB
Diamond Jubilee
(1928–1988)

Hodder & Stoughton
LONDON SYDNEY AUCKLAND TORONTO

Frontispiece: PK 6127 M (20,101 FT), *South Parbati valley. The southwest ridge dividing the south and west faces (Geoff Cohen).*

British Library Cataloguing in Publication Data

Mehta, Soli
    Exploring the hidden HImalaya.
    1. Himalayas. Mountaineering
    I. Title   II. Kapadia, Harish
    796,5′22′0954

    ISBN 0-340-50449-8

First published in Great Britain 1990

Published by Hodder and Stoughton,
a division of Hodder and Stoughton Ltd,
Mill Road, Dunton Green, Sevenoaks, Kent TN13 2YA.
Editorial Office: 47 Bedford Square, London WC1B 3DP.

Book designed by Trevor Spooner

Photoset by Rowland Phototypesetting Ltd,
Bury St Edmunds, Suffolk

Printed in Hong Kong

FOREWORD

by George Band
President of The Alpine Club

A S A Life Member of the Himalayan Club and currently also from the privileged position of President of the world's oldest mountaineering club – the Alpine Club in London – it gives me great pleasure to congratulate Soli Mehta and Harish Kapadia on producing this volume commemorating the Himalayan Club's Diamond Jubilee 1928–1988.

From their vantage point as Editors of the *Himalayan Journal* and the *Himalayan Club Newsletter*, and also from the experience of their own numerous expeditions, they are in a unique position to assemble and select photographs and material from some of the less publicised 6000 m and 7000 m peaks of the Indian Himalaya which still present exciting targets and challenges for both top ranking and more modest expeditions.

Age and time are no barrier. The authors recall the unnamed hero, a khalasi of the Survey of India, who carried a survey pole to the summit of Shilla, long thought to be an altitude record at 23,064 ft, but since downgraded to a mere 20,120 ft (6132 m).

Today's cheap flights now bring the Himalaya to one's doorstep. I was impressed that Chris Bonington and Jim Fotheringham could create a superb new route up the elegant granite spire of Shivling West (6501 m) in a week's holiday in 1983, after attending a conference in New Delhi.

There is scope for old age pensioners too, provided you have kept reasonably fit. Mike Banks (66) and Joss Lynam (62), a triple heart bypass surgery survivor, tackled a ridge on the east face of Jaonli (6632 m) this summer of 1989. Atrocious weather forced them to turn back, but I am looking forward to hearing their full story. Perhaps I can accompany them when they return to try again. I find it rather daunting that my own travels in the Indian Himalaya have not got beyond Sikkim, in the first chapter of this book; the attractions of Assam, Kumaon and Garhwal, Kishtwar, Kashmir and the eastern Karakoram – only recently reopened – still await me.

How does one select one's objectives for an expedition these days? Obviously, by reading this book, in conjunction with two other recent initiatives: the new map of the Mountains of Central Asia, scale 1:3 million, instigated by the Mount Everest Foundation and, secondly, by consulting the Alpine Club's Himalayan Index, a computerised database listing references from major mountaineering journals to all expeditions to peaks above 6000 m. This is probably the only way now to keep track of the 200 or more expeditions from all nations to the Himalaya each year.

Sadly, all these visitors don't just leave their footprints behind. Sir Edmund Hillary has decried the vast amounts of rubbish which litter the trail to the Everest Base Camp, now trod by some 5000 trekkers each year. In October 1987, I attended a unique gathering at Biella, in the Italian foothills below Mont Blanc, where mountaineers from all over the world discussed the problems of conserving 'Mountain Wilderness'. The conference gave unanimous support for 'clean' expeditions to the greater ranges which would completely burn, bury, eliminate or carry out all their refuse, instead of leaving it to disfigure the fragile mountain environment.

Fortunately the younger generation have a growing consciousness in this direction. Last night, as a temporary diversion from drafting this foreword, I performed on my home-made climbing wall and tutored a group of my son's friends who had really come just for barbeque, tennis and swimming. Who knows, I may have awakened in some of them the desire to visit those distant unknown valleys and peaks and so helped to create a deservedly wider readership ready for volume two of Mehta and Kapadia's *Exploring The Hidden Himalaya*.

George Band
Hartley Wintney, 1989

CONTENTS

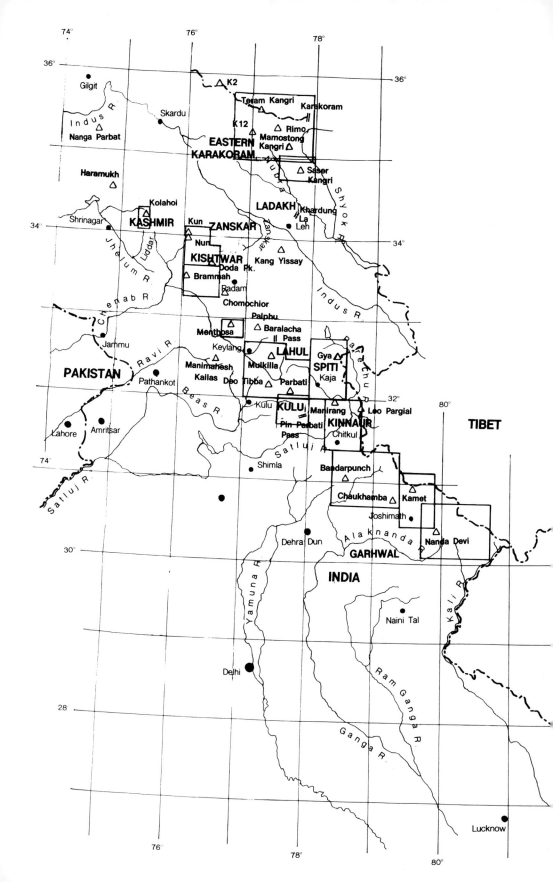

THE HIDDEN HIMALAYA

INDEX OF MAPS

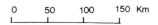

0   50   100   150 Km

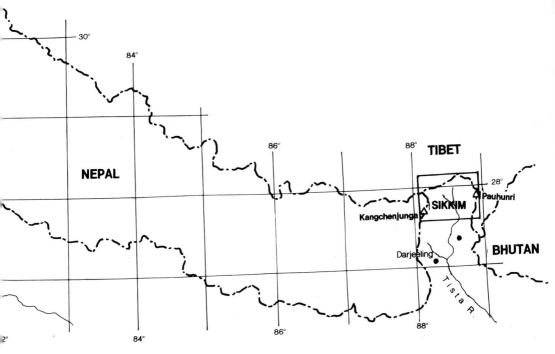

INTRODUCTION

I N 1988, the Himalayan Club celebrated its Diamond Jubilee. This publication is a special issue to commemorate the occasion.

In selecting what to include in this book we decided to avoid all 8000-metre peaks as having received enough attention elsewhere, and instead to highlight the lesser known peaks and climbing areas, while also describing some of the lesser known but challenging routes up the more famous mountains. We would outline the history of exploration and climbing in the areas we cover and update the main climbing activity to 1987–88. Bhutan, Nepal and the Western and Central Karakoram are not included since there have been, in recent years, a number of books covering these regions. Our main purpose is to excite the modern climber sufficiently for him to take notice of the vast possibilities the Himalaya has still to offer, to explore the little known paths, the unclimbed faces of known mountains and the hundreds of named and unnamed peaks to whom few have paid much attention. There has, however, been no attempt to turn this volume into a comprehensive dictionary of peaks in the Himalaya. Our problem has been not what to include, but what to leave out. The choice may perhaps appear to be a bit arbitrary, built up as it has been on the knowledge pooled from amongst our membership. Quite naturally, we have relied rather heavily on the issues of the *Himalayan Journal* and the *Himalayan Club Newsletters* for references. But should the reader fail to find his favourite peak or valley, we trust that he will be compensated by at least three that he has probably never heard of.

A word about the Club. The Himalayan Club was inaugurated in Delhi on 17 February 1928. Later in the year, on 14 December, an amalgamation took place with the Mountain Club, Calcutta. During the early years, the Club occupied itself by holding lectures, meetings and employing the specialists amongst its members to advise trekkers and climbers visiting the Himalaya on a variety of subjects such as geology, botany, zoology, and also render assistance to the large expeditions that visited the Himalaya and the Karakoram, by helping to clear baggage and equipment from the docks, hiring Sherpas and porters for them and offering the services of a liaison or transport officer to smooth over their trek to their base camp. In other ways, advice and equipment such as tents, sleeping bags etc., were ready at hand for any who sought them. The Sherpas were given numbers for identification and pass books for the comments of their employers to be entered. They were looked after by the local Secretary in Darjeeling who ensured that all got their fair share of expedition work. The Club started a tradition to award 'Tiger' badges for exemplary service from amongst the Sherpas. This was the picture of the Club around 1947–50.

The great surge in climbing activity after the war, the improvement in communications, the opening up of Nepal to foreigners, all helped in introducing mountaineering to the youth in India. From a small beginning, by the likes of Jack Gibson, Gurdial Singh, Holdsworth and John Martyn who took young schoolboys on summer trips to Garhwal, it progressed to the youngsters themselves (Nandu Jayal and Hari Dang for example) following in their school masters' footsteps. After the 1953 ascent of Everest by Edmund Hillary and Tenzing Norgay, Indian mountaineering burst out of its shell and within a decade mountaineering institutes were spawning climbers in large numbers, with sufficient interest generated amongst the youngsters to ensure the perpetuation of the sport by its own momentum.

With the proliferation of climbing clubs all over India and the formation of the Indian Mountaineering Foundation which issued permits and liaison officers to oversee the expeditions, the character of the Himalayan Club had perforce to change. Its assistance was no longer needed by large expeditions, Indian or foreign, as all of them were well-endowed with funds and experience to guide them to their goals.

The Club, however, does still carry out some of its traditional duties. It has a library, one of the finest on the Himalaya which may be consulted by members, and a scholarship fund to give financial assistance to Indian students attending courses at mountaineering institutes. It still maintains a fair amount of equipment at its main centres in India which is hired out to members at a nominal fee. It continues to hold meetings and seminars thus enabling the climbing fraternity in Bombay, Delhi, and Calcutta to meet and discuss their expeditions with slide shows and lectures. It provides information to many parties, both from India and abroad, and has amongst its members a great number of leading mountaineers, the world over.

Soon after its formation the Himalayan Club began the publication of the *Himalayan Journal* which after fifty-nine years of existence, has today come to be recognised as one of the foremost references to mountaineering and scientific activity in the Himalaya, Karakoram and the Hindu Kush. The *Journal* got off to a magnificent start with Kenneth Mason who nursed it from its humble beginnings to a mature publication. Logistic problems during the war and the retirement of its first editor brought forward the second generation, all of whom have authored books in their own right – Wilfrid Noyce, H. W. Tobin, George Band and Trevor Braham. With the departure of Trevor from India, there were some doubts whether this 'institution' could continue; but every crisis brings forth a hero and the *H.J.* survived by the induction of Dr K. Biswas, later assisted by John Martyn, both of whom held the fort and maintained the tradition with Bob Lawford pitching in for good measure – the crisis was over. It was easier for Soli Mehta to take over the reins and increase its coverage to the size that exists today. The person most responsible for the high standard of the current issues is Roy E. Hawkins. Hawk, as he is lovingly called by his friends, as Hon. Asst Editor introduced some consistency and refinement in the treatment of the material for publication which restored the *Journal*'s professionalism. In the years of Soli's absence from India, Harish Kapadia quickly learnt from Hawk and continued single-handed, innovating and improving further the presentation of material, both in the *H.J.* as well as the *Himalayan Club Newsletter* (*H.C.N.L.*) by roping in Dhiren Toolsidas, Arun Samant and Muslim Contractor.

Soli and Harish now continue as editors, and it was their idea of celebrating the Golden Jubilee with this special publication.

The photographic contributors have breathed the real life into this book. In all cases the photographs and slides were received without delay and where there was duplication, our choice became extremely difficult to make. From the hundreds received, we could select only a fraction of them and we take this opportunity to acknowledge our sincere thanks to all our friends and members who responded, whether their contributions are printed or not – we really have been overwhelmed by the generosity of thought and action from them.

A word about the authors who made all this possible. Firstly, we have Harish who along with Muslim Contractor dug up the horrendous amount of data from which the final material was sifted. They also wrote up the captions for the peaks and checked all factual data and references; the chapters on the Eastern Karakoram, Kinnaur, Spiti, Kashmir and Kumaon are edited from Harish's contributions some of which have been published in the *H.J.* The sketch maps are entirely the contribution of Arun Samant who has single-handedly solved that vexatious problem for us and, with the others, selected the colour and the black and white prints for publication. We were indeed lucky to have Joydeep Sircar for the chapter on the little known mountain area of Assam. The scant information must have been particularly difficult to extract. Soli Mehta undertook the task of researching Sikkim, Kulu-Lahul, Garhwal and editing all the other material for presentation in a uniform style.

We would wish the reader happy hunting; please share your unknown valleys and peaks with us – who knows, we might come out with a volume two.

Soli Mehta
Harish Kapadia
Honorary Editors,
The Himalayan Journal

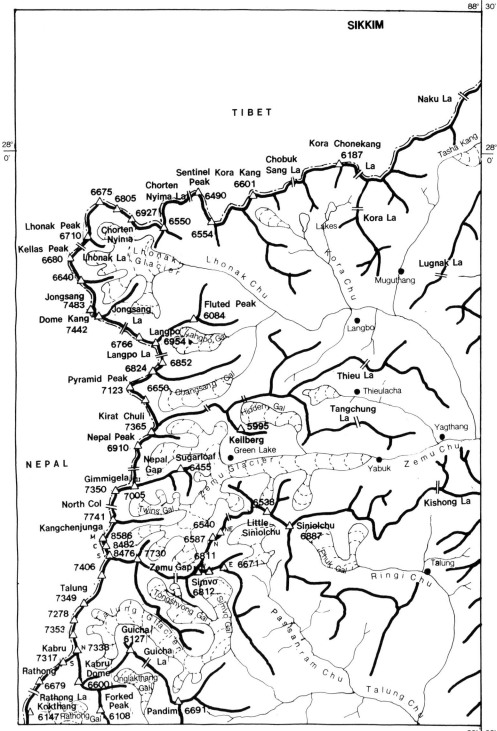

SIKKIM

T I B E T

NEPAL

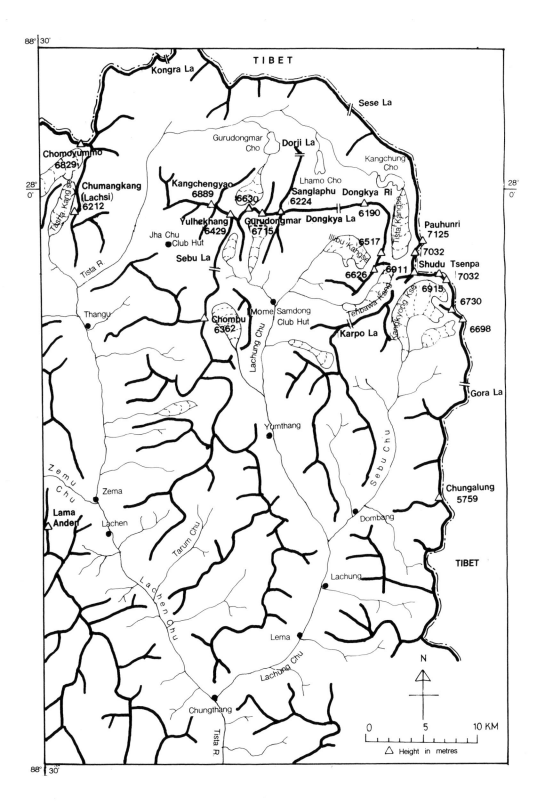

TIBET

Kongra La

Sese La

Gurudongmar Cho

Dorji La

Kangchung Cho

Chomoyummo
6829

Chumangkang
(Lachsi)
6212

Kangchengyao
6889

6630

Lhamo Cho

Sanglaphu
6224

Dongkya Ri

Yulhekhang
6429

Gurudongmar
6715

Dongkya La

6190

Pauhunri
7125

Jha Chu
Club Hut

Sebu La

Illibu Kangra

6517

7032

6626

6911

Shudu Tsenpa
7032

Thangu

Chombu
6362

Mome Samdong
Club Hut

Tehbawa Kang

6915

6730

Karpo La

6698

Lachung Chu

Gora La

Yumthang

Sebu Chu

Chungalung
5759

Zemu Chu

Zema

Dombang

Lama
Anden

Lachen

TIBET

Tarum Chu

Lachung

Lachen Chu

Lema

N

Chungthang

Lachung Chu

Tista R

0   5   10 KM

△ Height in metres

1
SIKKIM AND ASSAM HIMALAYA

SIKKIM

SIKKIM HIMALAYA is one of the more physically accessible sections of the Himalaya – within four days from Calcutta, the traveller can be among the mountains. In the records of exploration and climbing in Sikkim the names of Sir Joseph Hooker,[1] the great botanist explorer, Douglas Freshfield[2] and Dr A. M. Kellas[3] (eminent climbers of their day) stand out as having opened the western eyes to the beauty of the area and for calling attention to the possibilities of trekking and climbing of every degree of severity.

After the reconnaissance surveys under Hartman and Tanner which were completed in the 1870s, the country soon opened to travellers and explorers. Between 1888–96 Major L. A. Waddell made several journeys, although his book[4] is of greater interest to ethnologists.

Claude White also travelled extensively as Political Officer between 1889–1902. Amongst his travels, the more important were the ones in 1890 when he crossed the Guicha la and descended the Talung valley to the Tista river, becoming the first person to investigate the gorges between the Pandim and Simvo groups. His other major journey was up the Zemu glacier, to about 5340 metres. When stopped by bad weather, he diverted over the Thieu la into Lhonak where he was barred by the officious

Dzongpön of Kampa Dzong who claimed that the Thieu la was the frontier between Tibet and Sikkim. However after the 1902 Sikkim-Tibet boundary mission, White was able to travel further afield – all the way up the Chorten Nyima la.

In 1899, Freshfield, along with Prof Garwood, the brothers Sella and Sherpa Rinzin Namgyal, made his 'high-level' tour so interestingly described in his *Round Kangchenjunga*. He first traversed the Zemu glacier and camped east of the Green Lake (which, alas, has disappeared today – presumably drained when its blockage gave way). Bad weather foiled his attempts at investigating the approaches to the Nepal Gap and the Zemu Gap. He therefore crossed into Lhonak via the Thieu la, crossed the Jongsang la onto the Kangchenjunga glacier (in Nepal) and made a thorough study of the 'Pyramid', 'Tent' (now Kirat Chuli) and 'Nepal' peaks from the west. From the village of Kangbachen, he passed through Ghunsa and Tseram and re-crossed into Sikkim via the Kang la to Dzongri, whence he visited the Guicha la.

1883 was the year in which the first serious climbing began in Sikkim. The climber was W. W. Graham who, with two Swiss guides climbed Jubonu (5936 m), south of Pandim. He pronounced Pandim itself to be 'quite inaccessible owing to hanging glaciers', then proceeded to climb a mountain which he claimed was Kabru – that too in three days from a camp at 5640 m (18,500 ft) apparently by its southeast face. This ascent excited considerable controversy, with the various experts arguing for and against the claim. The most generous conclusion suggested that he had climbed Forked Peak (6108 m).

The first serious attempt on Kabru (7338 m) was made twenty-four years later in 1907 by Rubenson and Aas, two Norwegians, who approached their goal from the Rathong Chu and attacked the icefall between Rathong and the Kabru Dome. Five days of hard route-finding over the highly crevassed icefall brought them to the easier 'snow flat' (that can be seen from Darjeeling), whence they attempted the north summit (7338 m). The first attempt failed because of a late start and intense cold. The second time they tried from a higher camp, but once again the cold delayed their start and they gave up at about 7285 m. During the descent Rubenson slipped but was held by Aas (five of the six strands of the rope having broken under the strain). Frostbite to Aas' toes put paid to further attempts and the peak remained unclimbed till 1935 when C. R. Cooke succeeded in reaching its north summit.[5]

No climber has enjoyed himself and travelled so extensively in the Sikkim Himalaya as Dr A. M. Kellas. Unfortunately for the climbing fraternity he wrote hardly any detailed descriptions of his climbs. He first visited Sikkim in 1907 and then returned in 1909, 1910, 1912, 1920 and 1921. During 1907 he concentrated on the Zemu glacier, attempted Simvo with alpine guides, all three attempts being beaten back by bad weather and snow conditions. He also failed to reach the Nepal Gap in the two attempts made. In 1909 he attempted Pauhunri (7125 m) twice but was beaten back by storm and snow. He also visited the Langpo and Kangchenjunga glaciers, crossed the Jongsang la into Lhonak, reached high on Jongsang and climbed Langpo (6954 m). He tried for the Nepal Gap again, but was defeated near the top by a snowstorm.

The next year (1910) he returned to the Zemu and reached but did not cross the Simvo Saddle and the Zemu Gap. On his fourth attempt he at last reached the Nepal Gap, except for a small rock wall at the summit. He then crossed the 'Lhonak pass' into Lhonak and climbed high on Langpo to reconnoitre the summit of Jongsang, then crossed the Chorten Nyima la and climbed Sentinel Peak (6490 m) and finally dashed off to climb Pauhunri, which he did in a five-day struggle, and put the finishing touches to a most eventful season by climbing Chomoyummo (old spelling is Chomiomo) (6829 m) after reconnoitring its various approaches. His 1912 visit was devoted to exploration of the different approaches to Kangchengyao (6889 m) and he eventually reached the summit plateau from the north. He was believed to have been the first European to cross the Sebu la, connecting the Lachen and the Lachung valleys. He was back in 1920 and climbed Narsingh (5825 m). The following year he worked out a new route on the icefall of Kabru, hoping to use it later. He returned to Darjeeling only a few days before starting on the first British Everest expedition; alas, he died on his way through Tibet with the party.

One of the better documented journeys into Lhonak was that of G. B. Gourlay[6] who, with W. Eversden, managed to escape the heat of an October in Calcutta in 1930 to travel extensively in Lhonak.

Earlier that year (1930), the International expedition led by Prof G. O. Dyhrenfurth had not succeeded in its attempt on Kangchenjunga from the northwest (Nepal) side.[7,8] But the strong team of climbers, at their fittest after their struggle at altitude, engineered a route up and over the Nepal Gap. As the rest of the expedition worked its way slowly down the Lhonak valley to Lachen, E. Schneider climbed Nepal Peak (6910 m) by himself from the Gap. Then the remaining fit mountaineers crossed the Jongsang la into Lhonak and made the first ascent of Jongsang (7483 m) after gaining the north ridge (3 and 8 June, 1930). Schneider and Hoerlin, who were first up Jongsang, travelled on to the northern boundary with Tibet and climbed a high peak on the border.

One of the earliest traverses of the Passanram and Talung valleys was made by Dr E. Allwein and H. Pircher, members of the second unsuccessful German expedition to Kangchenjunga in 1931 (led by Paul Bauer). During the expedition, Allwein and Breuner had already ascended Sugar Loaf (6455 m). After the expedition disbanded these two, along with three Sherpas, climbed up to the Simvo Saddle (between Simvo and Siniolchu), hardly an easy route out of the Zemu glacier, and descended into the Passanram valley. Their journey[9] through miles of twisted rhododendron thicket, complicated by an inaccurate map, gave them a harrowing time before they emerged into the Talung valley and eventual habitation.

In 1932 G. A. R. Spence and J. Hale attempted Chomoyummo.[10]

Almost during the same period Capt G. H. Osmaston, along with friends, visited Lhonak over the Lugnak la,[11] and made an unsuccessful attempt on Fluted Peak (6084 m). Then the party visited the Chorten Nyima la and fixed accurately the position of Sentinel Peak, first climbed by Dr Kellas in 1910. On the way back Osmaston and his cousin entered the Zemu valley by a snow gap, Kellas' 'Lhonak Pass', four miles east of Kirat Chuli (Tent Peak), and from Yagthang, Osmaston proceeded alone over the Kishong la past the Talung monastery to Mangen. A pleasant month's holiday from Calcutta.

Lhonak in the days before the second world war was fast becoming a popular climbing area and, as the members from the two Kangchenjunga expeditions enjoyed the climbing in the valley, so the British climbers returning from Everest in 1933 chose to relieve their tired limbs on the lesser but by no means easier heights in Sikkim. Thus, Shipton and Wager crossed over from the Lashar plains into Lhonak over an unidentified pass which they named Lhonak la (first crossing) between the Jongsang and Lhonak Peaks.[12] From here, Shipton climbed Lhonak Peak (second ascent) to the north of the col.

G. B. Gourlay and J. B. Auden spent the October/November of 1934 in northeast Sikkim.[13] In spite of the wind and cold they took a lot of photographs and sorted out some of the inconsistencies in the Survey of India maps.

One of the more interesting climbs in the mid-thirties was C. R. Cooke's first ascent of Kabru in November 1935. He correctly predicted the more stable but colder weather conditions of the post-monsoon period as being the most suitable for Sikkim. G. Schoberth, six Sherpas and Cooke ascended the formidable icefall that guards all approaches from the east, under the slopes of the Dome. Once fully stocked in the relative safety of the upper terrace, which took them a good three weeks, they made rapid progress diagonally up the south face to reach the north summit in good order – a more successful repetition of the Norwegian attempt twenty years earlier.

Sikkim in 1936 was again a happy hunting ground for climbers and trekkers. The Germans (Paul Bauer) in preparation for Nanga Parbat (1937) visited the Zemu glacier with Karl Wien, A. Göttner and G. Hepp.[14] Their first attempts were on the eastern summit of the Twins (now Gimmigela) (7005 m) and yet another shot at Tent Peak (now Kirat Chuli) (7365 m), both beaten back by dangerous snow conditions, though they once again climbed Nepal Peak (6910 m) en route to Tent Peak. But a most satisfying climb was Siniolchu (6887 m) – one of the loveliest peaks in all Himalaya – by Wien and Göttner. Before leaving the region, Bauer, Göttner and Hepp climbed the western of the two north peaks of the Simvo massif (6587 m).

The same year Shipton, Warren, Kempson and Wigram, returning from Everest, entered Sikkim over the Kongra la and, from a camp on the nearby lake, Shipton and Kempson climbed Gurudongmar (6715 m).[15]

Meanwhile, Tilman ('with some unexpected time on my hands') pottered around the southern approaches to the Zemu Gap[16] and came away suitably chastened. This is by no means a recommended short cut into the Zemu glacier from Darjeeling.

The *Himalayan Journal* Vol. IX printed photographs, and noted the completion of the Himalayan Club hut at Mome Samdong. It was planned to build a similar hut on the Lachen side, enabling travellers to traverse the Lachung and Lachen valleys (over the Sebu la) without the use of tents. The second hut was subsequently established and the system worked admirably for a few years until the end of World War II, but neglect and disuse brought the facility to a sad end.

Kirat Chuli (old Tent Peak) (7365 m) continued to evade the most determined efforts – its armoury comprised soft and wind-slab snow and fierce winds. In 1937 Schmaderer, Paidar and Grob spent six weeks in the Zemu investigating the approaches to Kangchenjunga, during the course of which they had a shot at Tent Peak and the Twins, but were beaten back. As a consolation they made a fine second ascent of Siniolchu.

Later that year John Hunt with his wife and C. R. Cooke spent October/November in the Zemu.[17] They too had their eyes on Tent Peak. As they reached the ridge south of Nepal Peak, the wind smacked them with full force. Hunt bravely soloed up the western summit of Nepal Peak (only thirty-five metres below the main summit) before the sheer threat of being lifted off his feet by the wind persuaded him to return to the safety of the lower and protected heights. Cooke then led an exploration to the North Col of Kangchenjunga, Hunt reached Nepal and Zemu Gaps, and the party climbed Keilberg, a look-out peak just above Green Lake. They also crossed the Twins-Sugar Loaf ridge from the Nepal Gap glacier onto the Twins glacier – a remarkable feat. Finally Cooke left the Zemu over the Simvo Saddle and was lucky enough to chance on a relatively easier trail through the rhododendron jungle down the Passanram and Talung valleys to Mangen.

Another Everester returning from Tibet broke slightly newer ground. Naku la is a pass lying west of Chomoyummo and is used by Tibetans grazing their sheep along the Chaka Chu on the Sikkim side. Tilman, in 1938, followed this route into Lhonak, crossed over a col into the Tashi Chu and made the first ascent of Lachsi (6212 m). Having reached Thangu in the Lachen valley, he diverted into the Zemu, and made the only recorded crossing over the Zemu Gap, across the Tongshyong and Talung glaciers and over the Guicha la into the Parek Chu, Dzongri and back to civilisation – this crossing was more of a mountaineering feat than mere trekking and, from its description,[18] hardly to be recommended.

Kirat Chuli (Tent Peak) eventually allowed its first ascent in 1939[19] by Paidar, Schmaderer and Grob, who took the traditional route, over the top of Nepal Peak and reached the summit by the tricky and dangerous southwest ridge (29 May, 1939).

In July 1945, Harry Tilly climbed Chomoyummo (6829 m) and in September of the same year Wilfrid Noyce climbed Pauhunri (7125 m). Both were accompanied by Sherpa Angtharkay, and both were second ascents of peaks climbed by Dr A. M. Kellas.

Sikkim continued to be the favourite area for treks and short mountaineering holidays during the war years and after. The maps still appeared to contain errors, but one by one these were being put right by the keen members of the Himalayan Club – Trevor Braham in 1949 cleared some uncertainties in an area south of Pauhunri and discovered a 'hidden col' from the plateau at the head of the Kangkyong glacier to the valleys to the west and eventually into the Lachung valley, near Mome Samdong. His attempt on Kangchengyao by Kellas' 1912 route was beaten back by the lateness of the season (November), the chill of the winter winds and lack of what we today recognise as thermal protection. A real pioneering bit of work.[20]

In the early fifties, Sikkim began to receive its first set of geographical restrictions, particularly for foreigners, and gradually with the deterioration in the Indo-Chinese relationship, the flight of the Dalai Lama and the Indo-Sikkimese Treaty where the defence of Sikkim fell to India, permission even to Indian nationals became restricted in certain areas, mainly around the border passes into Tibet. Expeditions needed greater preparation and took longer to obtain permits beyond the Inner Line and mountaineering activity became restricted to teams from the Armed Forces. Eventually, around 1961, all but the small area of Western Sikkim was closed to everyone except Army personnel.

It was in 1975 that members of the Indian Air Force and the Indian Mountaineering Foundation (A. J. S. Grewal) attempted Talung from the Guicha la and Talung glacier.[21] Whilst the approach from the Sikkim side was peppered with avalanches and hanging glaciers, it was considered advisable to make serious attempts only from the Yalung glacier in Nepal. Attempts at reaching the Zemu Gap from the south were barred by large crevasses a few hundred feet below the saddle.

In 1976 Harish Kapadia and Zerksis Boga were the first civilians in fifteen years to be allowed into the north,[22] the playground of the past. They repeated some of the popular routes: to Green Lake, over the Thieu la into Lohnak, over the Lugnak la to Thangu, over the Sebu la to Mome Samdong and back to Chungthang.

Since then, most expeditions have been around the east Rathong glacier, the valley used by the students of the Himalayan Mountaineering Institute at Darjeeling. The usual targets are Frey Peak, Forked Peak, Kokthang and Kabru Dome. Rathong has been climbed by Indian pre-Everest expeditions and Army teams in 1964 and 1987, but always by the western approach, from the Yalung glacier.

In 1979,[23] a Calcutta based club was given permission to attempt Pandim (6691 m) and Guicha Peak (6127 m), both considered holy and therefore hitherto out-of-bounds – that is when the powers-that-be wanted to say 'No'. In the days when Sikkim was an independent Protectorate of the Indian Government, there used to be some consistency in the summits that were regarded as holy and therefore not open for climbing. They approached Pandim by trying to latch onto its north ridge from the Onglakthang glacier, but bad weather and lack of sufficient time forced them to return from a few metres short of the saddle on the ridge. The ridge connecting Guicha Peak and the Guicha la was deemed an unpromising route to the summit of Guicha due to snow conditions.

The same year Sonam Wangyal (Everest summitter, 1965) led a team from the Sikkim Police to Siniolchu[24] and the ascent was by more or less the same route as its two previous ascents in 1936 and 1937. A brave effort and a successful one over a heavily corniced and broken ridge connecting the summit with Little Siniolchu.

After considerable wrangling, permission was given to another Calcutta team in 1980 to climb Lama Anden, first climbed by Wing Cdr A. J. M. Smyth in 1944. Led by B. Nayak, their route lay over Kishong la and the ridge connecting the pass to the summit.[25] That this obvious route is not plain sailing was made quite clear to the team who had to retreat from fairly near the top owing to shortage of time and some error in route-finding.

Peaks to the north are still 'Armed Forces Territory'. Thus Gurudongmar (6715 m) was climbed from the northeast by an Assam Rifles party led by Norbu Sherpa in 1980,[26] forty-four years after its first ascent by Shipton and Kempson.

The following year a team from Bombay (sponsored by the Himalayan Club) attempted Kabru Dome,[27] a peak that looks far more easy than it actually is. For a start it is defended by an icefall that is extremely tricky, then comes the final badly broken ridge with several false summitlike bumps, and the highest point, at the far end of a wide arc, is sufficiently exposed to test the skill and endurance of the hardiest climber. Instead of attempting the normal icefall, they sought out a gully which gave them direct access to the ridge south of the peak. The gully too turned out to be a mini-icefall in disguise and, after some valiant attempts at getting through, they were forced to withdraw.

Yet another I.M.F.-sponsored pre-Everest expedition, led by Col D. K. Khullar, climbed Kabru Dome by the regular icefall route in 1982.[28]

The same year Sonam Wangyal led a successful Sikkim Police expedition to Lama Anden,[29] but his account in the *H.J.* Vol.39 is surprisingly bereft of even the most elementary detail of route.

Lama Anden was also climbed by an Indian Artillery team led by Lt Col Kuldip Singh in 1984.[30] A good effort that culminated in success after taking some risks through an avalanche-prone route.

Chomoyummo was climbed in 1986, this time by a pre-Kangchenjunga team from Assam Rifles.[31] A route from the northeast was selected. This was a mass ascent with a vengeance – a total of thirty-nine climbers reached the top in three summit groups on 27, 28 and 29 October, 1986.

Rathong was again a target for a Gurkha Rifles team in 1987. Led by Maj K. V. Cherian they vainly tried the approach from the east Rathong glacier. But after overcoming the horrible icefall, they found their way totally barred from the plateaulike amphitheatre that is surrounded by the peaks of Kabru and Kabru Dome. Learning their lesson, they then crossed over the saddle between Rathong and Kokthang into the Yalung valley taking the route of previous ascents, a fine west ridge that guides the climber to the summit which they reached on 24 May, 1987.[32]

Kokthang (6147 m), lying across the pass south of Rathong, has been claimed by several expeditions. Its serrated summit ridge comprises several humps, giving the impression of summits. An Army team (Maj Rana) in 1961, a ladies' expedition (Miss Pushpa Athavle) in 1966, another Army expedition (Maj K. V. Cherian) in 1986 and a Doon School team (Dr S. C. Biala), plus a team from Assam in 1988, have all reached subsidiary points on the ridge while the true summit at its northernmost end remains inviolate.

SIKKIM REFERENCES

1 *Himalayan Journals* Vols.I & II, J. Hooker, 1854; also *H.J.* Vol.XVI, p.86.
2 *Round Kangchenjunga,* Douglas W. Freshfield, London, 1903.
3 *H.J.* Vol.II, p.1.
4 *Among the Himalayas,* L. A. Waddell, 1899.
5 *H.J.* Vol.VIII, p.107.
6 *H.J.* Vol.IV, p.123.
7 *H.J.* Vol.III, p.77.
8 *The Kangchenjunga Adventure,* Frank Smythe, London, 1932.
9 *H.J.* Vol.V, p.58.
10 *Ibid.* p.94.
11 *Ibid.* p.108.
12 *H.J.* Vol.VI, p.51.
13 *H.J.* Vol.VII, p.139.

14 *H.J.* Vol.IX, p.58.
15 *Ibid.* p.156.
16 *Ibid.* p.95.
17 *H.J.* Vol.X, p.49.
18 *H.J.* Vol.XI, p.147.
19 *H.J.* Vol.XIII, p.46.
20 *H.J.* Vol.XVI, p.74.
21 *H.J.* Vol.XXXIV, p.39.
22 *H.J.* Vol.XXXV, p.181.
23 *H.J.* Vol.37, p.42.
24 *Ibid.* p.51.
25 *Ibid.* p.173.
26 *H.J.* Vol.38, p.156.
27 *Ibid.* p.20.
28 *H.J.* Vol.39, p.156.
29 *Ibid.* p.159.
30 *H.J.* Vol.41, p.140.
31 *H.C.N.L.* 41, p.26.
32 *H.J.* Vol.44, p.48.

1 PANDIM (6691 M)
A sacred and famous peak in West Sikkim. W. W. Graham recceed it in 1883 followed by H. Boustead in 1926, and T. H. Somervell in 1928. It was seriously explored by C. R. Cooke and John Hunt in 1940, before it was closed for religious reasons. In recent years it has beaten back two attempts but the sacred mountain still remains a virgin challenge.

2 KANGCHENGYAO (6889 M)
Kangchengyao lies in the Dongkya range in Sikkim, north of the Sebu la. It was first attempted by Dr Kellas in 1912. He approached from the north, gained the east col and then reached the east summit which is slightly lower than the main or western peak.
Discounting a dubious claim in 1961, the first ascent of the main peak was made in 1982 by an Indian Army team (Maj V. Singh).

1 PANDIM *from Chemathang (Dorjee Lhatoo).*

2 KANGCHENGYO *southeast face (Harish Kapadia).*

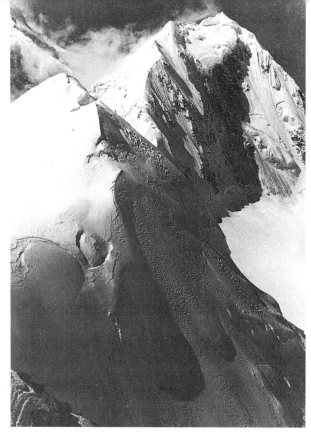

3 GIMMIGELA (TWINS) (7350 M)

Situated above the North Col of Kangchenjunga, this pair of peaks was first recceed by Paul Bauer's team in 1936 from the Twins glacier. They attempted the eastern peak unsuccessfully. A Japanese attempt in 1963 reached within 200 m of one of the summits before withdrawing in bad weather.

3 GIMMIGELA *(Twins) from the west ridge of Sugar Loaf (John Hunt).*

4 KIRAT CHULI *(Tent Peak) from Sugar Loaf (John Hunt).*

4 KIRAT CHULI (7365 M)

Formerly known as 'Tent Peak', Kirat Chuli is a prominent peak on the ridge running north from Kangchenjunga. Paul Bauer's team made an attempt on the southwest ridge in 1936, passing over the summit of Nepal Peak (6910 m) but gave up due to dangerous avalanches. Next year, a German-Swiss team was beaten back, as were C. R. Cooke and John Hunt, the latter reaching the southwest summit of Nepal Peak. The same German-Swiss team made a fine first ascent in 1939. Approaching from the Nepal Gap, they climbed Nepal Peak and then followed the difficult 1.5 km ridge leading to Kirat Chuli. The next attempt was in 1985, from Nepal, by a British-Nepal expedition but this failed on the south ridge of Nepal Peak. Other routes remain to be tried.

5 SINIOLCHU (6887 M)
Rising on the southern side of the Zemu glacier on the watershed between the Passanram and the Zemu glaciers, Siniolchu has often been labelled the most beautiful peak in the world. It was first climbed by Paul Bauer's team in 1936. From their base on the Zemu glacier, they reached the ridge between Siniolchu and Little Siniolchu (6538 m) and climbed it to the summit. The second ascent was made the next year by a German-Swiss expedition, while the third ascent was achieved by an Indian team in 1979.

5 SINIOLCHU *from the Zemu glacier (Paul Bauer).*

6 KABRU DOME *looking at the southwest face from the East Rathong glacier (Soli Mehta).*

6 KABRU DOME (6600 M)
The first ascent was made in 1982 by an Indian team (Col D. K. Khullar) which followed the glacier between the Dome and Forked Peak. It also has a peculiar trait of being declared sacred and thus out of bounds for climbers in some years, while in others large groups trample all over it with official blessings – one of the few man-made mysteries in the Himalaya.

7 CHOMBU (6362 M)
Chombu lies on the ridge separating the Lachen and Lachung valleys in northeast Sikkim. It was recceed by a British team in 1944 from two different sides from the Himalayan Club hut at Jha Chu and again in 1952 by T. H. Braham. It was reported to be climbed by an Indian team in 1961, but this is widely disbelieved. A definite ascent of this peak is yet to be established.

8 KABRU (S PEAK – 7317 M; N PEAK – 7338 M)
This prominent pair of peaks lie on the continuation of the Kangchenjunga-Talung ridge in the Singalila range. They are approachable from the Rathong as well as the Talung glaciers. A Norwegian pair made a spirited attempt from the Rathong glacier and after crossing the huge icefall

7 CHOMBU *looking southeast from Sebu (Harish Kapadia).*

proceeded along the ridge joining the two summits but were beaten by the cold and the wind when just about 50 m below the north summit. This was a pioneering post-monsoon attempt. In 1935 C. R. Cooke was successful even later (November) and made the first ascent of the north peak. He reached the summit alone. This climb has not been repeated while Kabru South awaits its first ascent.

9 KOKTHANG (6147 M)
The peak lies across a col south of Rathong. Its serrated summit ridge has led almost all the expeditions to believe that they have reached the

summit. All have reached one or other of the subsidiary humps on the ridge, while the true high point, lying at the northernmost end, remains to be climbed.

10 SIMVO (6812 M)
East of the Zemu Gap stands Simvo with its four subsidiaries – West (6811 m), East (6671 m), North (6587 m) and Northeast (6540 m). The north peak was first climbed by Paul Bauer's team in 1936 from the Zemu glacier. Two Indian teams have made ascents of what is presumed to be the main peak, one in 1979, the other in 1984. Details of both ascents, however, are lacking.

8 KABRU SOUTH *from Rathong Col (Dorjee Lhatoo).*

9 KOKTHANG *from its north saddle. True Peak is the high point on extreme left (Soli Mehta).*

10 *Four peaks of* SIMVO *from Zemu glacier (Paul Bauer).*

ASSAM HIMALAYA

T HE TERM Assam Himalaya was originally ap-
plied to the entire Himalayan chain stretching
eastwards from Pauhunri (7125 m) to Namcha
Barwa (7762 m). Time has rendered this nomenclature obsolete; the portion of the range lying mainly in
Bhutan is now correctly called Bhutan Himalaya, and the
erstwhile mega-province of Assam has lost its Himalayan
frontier to Arunachal Pradesh, recently born out of what
was the North-Eastern Frontier Agency (N.E.F.A.). So,
properly speaking, there is no longer any Assam Himalaya.
But anachronism though it is, the term is familiar and
hallowed by long usage, and till geographers come up with
an acceptable alternative, little harm will be done if the
range between the transverse valley of the Manas above
Tawang and the great bend of the Tsangpo around the giant
pivot of the Namcha Barwa massif continues to be called
Assam Himalaya. The mountains beyond the Tsangpo-
Dihang are not considered part of the Himalaya, which
leaves Gyala Peri (7150 m) and the 6000-metre Nyimo
Chomo range out of our reckoning.[1]

For the major part of its length, the Assam Himalaya is a
low range by Himalayan standards, between 5000 and 6000
metres high, and devoid of much mountaineering interest.
There are two significant exceptions to this. One, as already
mentioned, is the Namcha Barwa section. The position and
height of this 'mysterious giant' was determined by British
expeditions operating in the Abor and Mishmi tribal areas
only as recently as 1912, although its existence had been
reported more than forty years earlier by the pandit explorers. The following year it was approached and surveyed
by Morshead during his exploration of the Tsangpo with
Bailey. They also discovered Gyala Peri during this expedition.[2] After a prolonged period of neglect, caused by geographical and political inaccessibility, Namcha Barwa was
strongly recceed by a Chinese team in 1983;[3] permission to
climb has been under negotiation for some time, by the
Japanese.[4] No doubt we can look forward to more climbs in
this area.

The other zone of mountaineering interest is the least known of all Himalayan areas. Visible from the distant plains of Assam and the Meghalaya hills, from where it was surveyed, the high range of the Kangto section lies in a gigantic S-curve running roughly west-southwest and east-northeast between the passes of the Tulung la and Keshong la. The McMahon line runs more or less along the crest, and to the south spread the high, rain-sodden, thickly forested spurs and ridges of the lesser Himalaya, impeding access from the Assam plains. The approach from Tibet is relatively easier.

Inhabited by less than friendly tribals, the area had little allure except to hardy botanists and ethnologists up till the end of the thirties. Post-independence Indian penetration and permanent occupation of this zone (the Balipara Frontier Tract of the empire days) may have been expected to improve accessibility, but the 1962 border war put paid to such 'civilian' hopes. Though roads have been built and detailed mapping done, these mountains remain as pristine and remote as of yore behind the ring wall of the Official Secrets Act.

What follows are just a few facts we have been able to gather about the major named peaks of the Kangto section. Though they are scanty, we hope that the curiosity aroused could eventually lead to more relaxations for travel in this forgotten area.

Gori Chen (6538 m)

This is the most westerly of the major peaks of the Kangto section, and has received most attention due to its proximity to inhabited localities to its south and west. While descending to Assam after surveying the range from the north in 1913, F. M. Bailey and H. T. Morshead crossed the Tulung la to the border hamlet of Mago. From there they reached Lap (4420 m) on the upper Gorjo Chu, a tributary of the Manas. The Gorjo Chu rises beneath Gori Chen and is the natural approach route to the peak. From Lap, they continued across the Tse la (4724 m) and the Poshing la (4115 m) to reach the Tembang village above Bomdila.[5] This somewhat unpopular Tibetan trading route thereafter acquired the unjustified sobriquet of 'the Bailey Trail'. The area was visited by F. Kingdon Ward, F. Ludlow, G. J. Sherriff et al, during the course of botanical expeditions in the thirties. However, no recce of Gori Chen was carried out.[6]

In 1939, that most-travelled of all mountaineers, H. W. Tilman, set out to recce the mountains of this area. The title he gave his report was *Assam Himalaya Unvisited*, with good reason. Accompanied by Sherpas Nukku, Wangdi Nurbu and Thondup, he set out from Charduar in Assam in April, and gamely struggled up the Bailey Trail to base camp at Lap, despite malaria which affected the entire team. Another camp was sited higher up the Gorjo Chu, and Tilman carried out some plane-tabling from stations between 4800 m and 5200 m but his hopes of crossing the headwall of the valley and breaking into the Gori Chen basin were dashed with the death of Nukku, of malaria, on 26 May.

Tilman felt that climbs in this range could be accomplished more easily from Tibet, but obtaining the necessary permission to do so from Lhasa would be difficult.[7] It should be a shade easier now than in Tilman's time.

In 1962 the Chinese Army came in strength down the Bailey Trail in a strategic stroke that destroyed the last Indian defences of western N.E.F.A.[8] As part of the resurgence of activity following the debacle, an Army expedition under T. Haralu set out in the autumn of 1966 for Gori Chen. The summit was reached on 29 October by Maj J. C. Joshi, Capt N. Thapa, Lt A. J. B. Jaini, Lt N. P. Rajagopal, Nk Mann Singh, L/Nk Darshan Singh, L/Nk Hira Bahadur and Gyamtsola.[9] Singularly little appears to have been written about this climb. The only account publicly available is a piece by Joshi dealing with a fall by his assault partners, Darshan and Rajagopal, while descending the difficult stretch below the summit. Joshi held them with difficulty, but both suffered serious frost injuries. It is surmised that the approach was up the Gorjo Chu valley.[10]

There is one more notable thing about this 1966 climb. The altitude of Gori Chen underwent an unexplained revision upwards from 6538 to *c*.6858 m. The latter figure is now being quoted without the 'circa'.

A rumoured plan by Assamese climbers to visit Gori Chen and Kangto in the early seventies came to nothing, and it was only after another twenty-one years that another Army team under Subhendu Sen set out for Gori Chen. Starting from Dzong (Jang) on the Gorjo Chu, they marched for five days to their base camp at 4709 m, then moved northwards to set up C1 (*c*.5180 m) and C2 (*c*.5790 m). Pk 6247 m lying south of Gori Chen was climbed on 19 October, 1987 by Lt Bajaj, Vinod Kumar, Sherpa Lakhpa, N. D. Sherpa, K. Singh, P. Singh, Hari Thapa, Hira Thapa and the leader.[11]

Kangto (7090 m)
Nothing is known about the attempts on or exploration of Kangto. Tilman believed that this peak was the same as the one called Shorkang Karbo by the people of Tombang.

Nyegyi Kangsang (7047 m)
This peak which lies northeast of Kangto has not been explored to date. The main difficulty is in obtaining permission to enter the area.

Takpa Shiri (6655 m)
This is a holy mountain just north of the border, near the Tibetan village of Migyitun. Its circumambulation gives religious merit, like that of Kailas, and both Bailey and Sherriff performed 'Kingkor', or the smaller pilgrimage, which takes about a week.[12] Although earlier maps gave the height quoted above, it is very likely that the peak is only about 5800 m high.

Apart from the named peaks mentioned here, there are a number of unnamed summits over 6000 m in the Kangto section. One of them is 6923 metres high. Here again, an opportunity to carry out much more detailed exploration exists, but accessibility here is a more serious problem than elsewhere in the Himalaya.

ASSAM HIMALAYA REFERENCES

1 *The Encyclopaedia of Mountaineering*, Walt Unsworth, London, 1975.
2 *Abode of Snow*, Kenneth Mason, p.44. London, 1955.
3 *H.C.N.L.* 38 p.4.
4 *H.J.* Vol.43, p.1.
5 *No Passport in Tibet*, F. M. Bailey.
6 *H.J.* Vol.VII, p.103; Vol.VIII, p.125; Vol.IX, p.144; Vol.X, p.1; Vol.XII, p.1.
7 *Alpine Journal*, Vol.52, 1940.
8 *India's China War*, N. Maxwell.
9 *Himalayan Mountaineering Journal*, Vol.4 No.2.
10 *Himalayan Association Journal*, Vol.I, 1970.
11 *Himavanta*, March, 1988.
12 *H.J.* Vol.IX, p.145; *ibid* Vol.X, p.9.

11 GORICHEN (6858 M)

One of the rarely seen peaks in the Pachaksiri range of the Assam Himalaya. An Indian team (T. Haralu) is reported to have climbed this peak in 1966. The second ascent was made by an Indian Army expedition (Maj A. Sen).

12 KANGTO (7090 M)

The Kangto range extends from Chayul Chu in the east to Kuru Chu in the west. The highest point on this range is Kangto. A recent attempt to reach this massif was thwarted in the thick jungles through which it has to be approached.

13 NYEGYI KANGSANG (7047 M)

This is the highest mountain in the Pachaksiri range of the Assam Himalaya, which extends from the Siyom on the northeast as far as the Chayul Chu to its south. No attempt has been made on this peak.

11 GORICHEN *(Romesh Bhattacharjee).*

12 KANGTO *(Romesh Bhattacharjee).*

13 NYEGYI KANGSANG *(Romesh Bhattacharjee).*

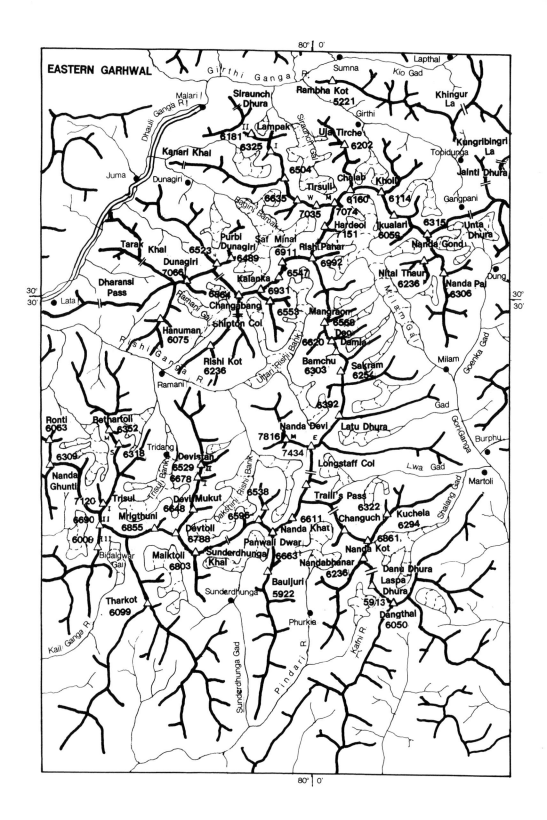

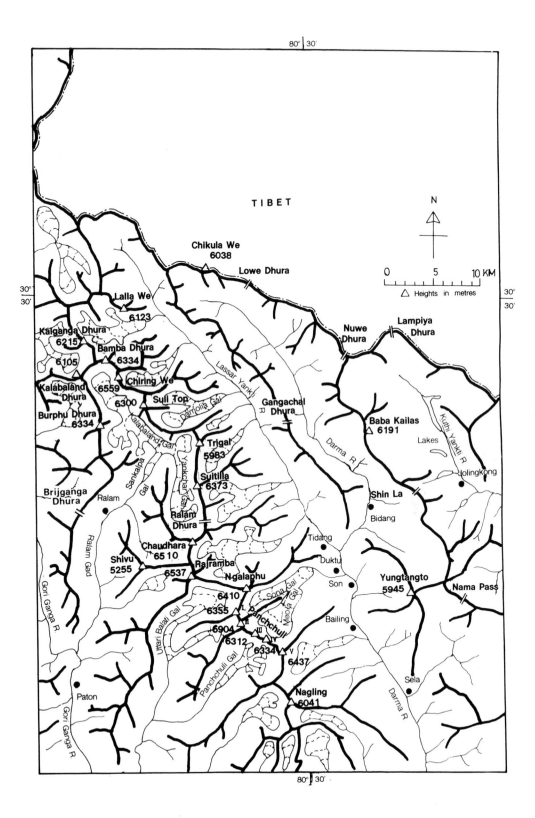

TIBET

Chikula We
6038

Lowe Dhura

N

0   5   10 KM

△ Heights in metres

30'
30'

Lalla We
6123

Nuwe
Dhura

Lampiya
Dhura

Kalganga Dhura
6215

6105

Bamba Dhura
6334

Lassar Yankti

Kalabaland
Dhura

Chiring We
6559

Gangachal
Dhura

Baba Kailas
6191

Lakes

Jolingkong

Suli Top
6300

Kalabaland Gal

Damola Gal

Burphu Dhura
6334

Darma R

Kuthi Yankti R

Sankalpa

Trigal
5983

Yankchar Gal

Suitilla
6373

Shin La

Brijganga
Dhura

Ralam

Ralam
Dhura

Bidang

Ralam Gad

Chaudhara
6510

Tidang

Shivu
5255

Rajramba
6537

Ngalaphu

Duktu

Yungtangto
5945

Nama Pass

Gori Ganga R

6410

Son

6355

I. Panchchuli
II

Sona Gal

Bailing

6904
III
IV

Medta Gal

6312

6334
V

6437

Uttari Balati Gal

Sela

Paton

Panchchuli Gal

Nagling
6041

Darma R

Gori Ganga R

2
KUMAON AND GARHWAL

KUMAON

KUMAON is often confused with the other parts of Garhwal – indeed there is no official border to demarcate the region. Its eastern boundary runs along the Kali river which separates India from Nepal. The tributaries, Kuthi, Darma and Lassar, flow into the Kali at different points. The Kali valley was once the standard trade route from India into Tibet over the Lipu Lekh pass.

The Kuthi emerges from Jolingkong Lake, as beautiful a spot as any, while other passes of Mangsha Dhura and Lampiya Dhura are not far away. Sangthang (6480 m) is the only peak known to have been climbed in this section – by an Indian team (P. Dasgupta).[1]

As we come westwards, we are aware of several excellent climbing areas. Let's take them one by one, east to west.

The Panchchuli massif has five summits (the five cooking pots on which the Pandavs cooked their last meal on their way to heaven). It forms the barrier between the Darma and Gori valleys. The summits are numbered north to south. Peak II at 6904 m is the highest. They were earlier attempted from the Sona and Meola glaciers in the east; H. Ruttledge recceed the mountain in 1929, Graaff and Snelson did likewise in 1950, as did the Scots, also in 1950. Heinrich Harrer and Frank Thomas, with Sherpas Gyalzen and Lhakpa, made an attempt from the west in 1952.[2] Finally the Indo-Tibet Border Police opened the route in 1972 and made the first ascent in 1973 from the west. The area is plastered with smaller peaks such as Nagling (6042 m).

The Gori valley has some excellent climbing prospects, too. Chiring We (6559 m), one of the finest, was climbed in 1979 by an Indian team (Harish Kapadia)[3] exploring in the Kalabaland glacier, a veritable amphitheatre of climbable summits. The same expedition also climbed Bamba Dhura (6334 m), Kalabaland Dhura (6105 m) and Pk 5928 m. The other peaks worthy of attention are Suli Top (6300 m), climbed by an Indian team (R. Mahadik);[4] to its south lies Suitilla (6373 m), unclimbed to date; lower down the same ridge Chaudhara (6510 m) was climbed by an Indian party (A. R. Chandekar)[5] in 1973 and Rajrambha (6537 m) ascended by the Indo-Tibet Border Police (I.T.B.P.) in 1971 – all subsequent attempts on it having failed.

The portion of Gori valley from Munsiary to Milam is known as Johar from the grain that is harvested in the non-trading season. A solid stone track leads over the Unta Dhura pass towards Tibet. At the head of this valley stand Hardeol (7151 m) and Tirsuli (7074 m) which have attracted many parties. The Poles attempted Tirsuli in 1939, failed and lost two members at C3.[6] In 1964 Lt Cdr M. S. Kohli's team got caught in an avalanche and K. P. Sharma's expedition was beaten back by blizzards and snow conditions. A determined bid by a Calcutta team led by Chanchal Mitra in 1966 finally made the first ascent.[7] Tirsuli's neighbour, Hardeol (God's Temple), has dealt just as severely with its earlier visitors, the most devastating blow being when four members of an Indo-New Zealand ladies' expedition were killed in an avalanche in the icefall not far from one of the camps. Finally a strong team of Sherpas of the I.T.B.P. (S. P. Mulasi) climbed over the ridge, traversing Pks 6600 m and 6805 m to the summit at 7151 m. A magnificent achievement by any standards.

At the eastern end of the same cirque lie Nanda Pal (6306 m), Nanda Gond (6315 m), Nital Thaur (6236 m) and Kalganga Dhura (6215 m) – each with enough technical difficulty to match its beauty. Only Nanda Pal has been climbed.

To the west of this arena stand the peaks of the Nanda

Devi Sanctuary along with the goddess herself. From here Longstaff reached the col named after him overlooking the Sanctuary. Nanda Kot (6861 m), Fort of Nanda, stands guard, dividing the Gori from the Pindari valleys. It was recceed in 1905 by Longstaff, but it was only in 1936 that the Japanese made its first ascent.[8] An Indian Navy team led by Lt M. S. Kohli made the second ascent in 1959,[9] and an Indo-Japanese expedition again climbed it in 1986 to celebrate the Golden Jubilee of its first ascent.

Danpur is the western region of Kumaon, so named from the generosity of its people (*Dan*, a gift, *pur*, place). Porters from this area are reportedly the best and most faithful. The area comprises the two major valleys of Pindari and Sunderdhunga.

The Pindari glacier ends at Traill's Pass at its head, with the peaks of Nanda Khat, Bed of Nanda (6611 m), to its north and Nanda Kot to its south. To the south of Pindari is the Kafni glacier at the head of which nestle the peaks of Nandabhanar (6236 m) and Nandakhani (6029 m).

Panwali Dwar, Gateway of Winds, (6663 m) is a beautiful peak on the outer wall of the Sanctuary, separating the Pindari from the Sunderdhunga. As on other peaks, the Japanese mounted a succession of expeditions until their single-mindedness was crowned with a successful ascent in 1980, thus completing all the major summits of the area.

Sunderdhunga, Beautiful Stones, certainly lives up to its name. Shipton and Tilman descended by the pass at its head from the Sanctuary in 1934; as an exit route they warned against its use and climbers have taken their advice. In 1944 Wilfrid Noyce[10] made the first ascent of Tharkot (6099 m), previously known as Simsaga; he also climbed Maiktoli (6803 m), and Bauljuri (5922 m), then known as South Maiktoli. Maiktoli had of course been climbed by Shipton in 1934. It has a formidable south face, an imposing 1800 m wall which was climbed in 1977 by the Japanese.

Adjoining the Sunderdhunga valley is the Bidalgwar glacier which affords a southern approach to the Trisul massif. The southern aspects of the Sanctuary have a lot to interest the cautious climber. One of the main objective dangers for visitors to this area is avalanches, a natural result of the south-facing terrain catching the brunt of the monsoon which is allowed to cause less damage to areas to the north by the Sanctuary walls.

KUMAON REFERENCES
1 *H.J.* Vol.XXX, p.161.
2 *H.J.* Vol.XVII, p.97; Vol.XVIII, p.171.
3 *H.J.* Vol.36, p.68.
4 *H.J.* Vol.43, p.33.
5 *H.J.* Vol.XXXIII, p.115.
6 *H.J.* Vol.XII, p.78.
7 *H.J.* Vol.XXVII, p.67.
8 *H.J.* Vol.X, p.71; Vol.XI, p.174.
9 *H.J.* Vol.XXIII, p.21.
10 *H.J.* Vol.XIII, p.95.

14 CHAUDHARA (6510 M)
This peak lies to the south of Ralam pass. Chaudhara, the Peak of Four Corners, was climbed by an Indian team (A. R. Chandekar), which included the famous Sherpa Ajeeba, in 1973.

15 PANCHCHULI V (6437 M)
This is the southernmost peak of the massif and the most formidable. The east ridge and the northeast face, seen here, offer climbing of the highest standard.
NAGLING *(6041 m), Snake's Head, is as difficult a climb as its neighbour. Imagine this view as seen from the rest house at Son Duktu.*

16 PANCHCHULI II (6904 M)
The five summits of this range lie on the Darmaganga-Milam divide. Panchchuli II is the highest of the group. It was recceed in 1929 by H. Ruttledge. The first attempt on this peak was by Heim and Gansser in 1937, followed by the Scottish Himalayan Expedition, by Graaff and Snelson in 1950 and by Heinrich Harrer in 1954. It was first climbed by an I.T.B.P. team in 1973 (M. Singh). The other peaks of the group are graceful in appearance with sharp flutings.

14 CHAUDHARA *from Kalabaland glacier (Harish Kapadia).*

16 PANCHCHULI II *from Munsiari (Harish Kapadia).*

15 PANCHCHULI V *(right) and* NAGLING *from Son Duktu (Harish Kapadia).*

17 *Left*, KALABALAND DHURA *and, right*, BURPHU DHURA, *from above the Kalabaland icefall (Harish Kapadia).*

18 TIRSULI *and* HARDEOL *from Brijganga Dhura in the Milam valley (Harish Kapadia).*

19 CHIRING WE, *west ridge, from Kalabaland Dhura (Harish Kapadia).*

20 SUITILLA *from the Kalabaland glacier (Harish Kapadia).*

21 CHANGUCH *from the Pindari glacier (Anup Sah).*

22 LASPA DHURA, *above the Kafni glacier (S. N. Dhar).*

23 PANWALI DWAR *from the Pindari glacier (Anup Sah).*

24 NILGIRI PARBAT *from the Bank Kund valley (Harish Kapadia).*

17 BURPHU DHURA (6334
M) *and* KALABALAND
DHURA (6105 M)
*Burphu Dhura, the
unclimbed Peak of Snows
on the Kalabaland-Milam
divide is a formidable
challenge, having beaten
back two expeditions. It has
approaches from the
Kalabaland glacier above
the icefall and also from the
steep face falling to Burphu
village in the Milam valley.
Kalabaland Dhura is at the
head of an icefall of the
same name. It was climbed
in 1979 by an Indian team
(Harish Kapadia).*

18 HARDEOL (7151 M)
and TIRSULI (7074 M)
*Hardeol, the Temple of
God, has only once allowed
climbers onto its summit.
Four members of an Indo-
New Zealand Ladies team
were killed in 1974 in its
lower icefall and it defeated
an I.T.B.P. team in 1975.
In 1978 the I.T.B.P. (S. P.
Mulasi) approached it from
the south. Climbing to over
6500 m on the Tirsuli
ridge, they went over a
satellite peak of c.6850 m
on the east ridge and,
descending to a col
separating it from the true*

*summit, made the first
ascent. The northeasterly
neighbour of Hardeol is
Tirsuli. Its history began in
1939 when two Poles
perished on it in an
avalanche; two Indian
attempts in 1964 and 1965
were unsuccessful. A repeat
visit by an Indian team
(Chanchal Mitra) in 1966
made the first ascent. The
route makes three traverses,
one on the Milam-Tirsuli
glacier and two on the
mountain's slopes.*

19 CHIRING WE (6559 M)
A shy peak at the head of the Kalabaland glacier. This Mountain of Long Life cannot be seen till the icefall is climbed. With a steeply rising face and sharp ridges it defends itself well. After an unsuccessful attempt in 1977, an Indian team (Harish Kapadia) returned in 1979 to make the first ascent from its northeast ridge. It has defeated two later expeditions. It offers many steep routes and the subsidiary peaks, Chiring We II and III, await climbers.

20 SUITILLA (6373 M)
Though small, this peak can be called the best piece of mountain architecture. With steep ice-flutings this Peak of Needles lies at the junction of Kalabaland, Yankchar and Sankalpa glaciers. It awaits an ascent.

21 CHANGUCH (6322 M)
Situated above the popular Pindari glacier, this peak has already beaten back two attempts and remains unclimbed. For the adventurous, it also offers a ridge leading to Nanda Kot (6861 m).

22 LASPA DHURA (5913 M)
One of three prominent peaks on the Kafni-Shalang divide, Laspa Dhura was first climbed by an Indo-British team (B. Mukhoty) in 1987. They approached via the Kafni glacier and placing a camp under the north ridge of Laspa Dhura, ascended it to the summit. The descent was made by the west ridge. This team also made the first ascents of Nandabhanar (6236 m) and Nandakhani (6029 m).

23 PANWALI DWAR (6663 M)
It is the Gateway of the Winds, rising above the Pindari glacier. W. Noyce observed it in 1944 but no attempts were made till the Japanese did so in 1979. They returned in 1980 to climb it (K. Nakae). Many different routes remain to be tried.

24 NILGIRI PARBAT (6474 M)
The Blue Mountain lies in Frank Smythe's favourite mountain area. He made the first ascent in 1937. The second ascent was in 1962 by an Indian team (A. Sen). Both were by the northwest ridge, and from the Khulia Garvya glacier. The route from the Amrit Ganga valley would give access to the east and north faces – both of which are really challenging.

25 NANDA DEVI EAST (7434 M) *and* LONGSTAFF COL (5910 M)
A rare high view of the Longstaff Col (depression in the foreground) and the long southern ridge of Nanda Devi East. Dr T. G. Longstaff reached the col from the east with two guides in 1905. H. W. Tilman and Charles Houston descended this in 1936 after their first ascent of Nanda Devi. Nanda Devi East was climbed in 1939 (Polish, A. Karpinski), 1951 (French, R. Duplat), 1975 (Indo-French, Y. Pollet-Villard) and 1976 (Indo-Japanese, K. Kano).

25 NANDA DEVI EAST *and* LONGSTAFF COL *(Mridul Bose)*.

26 NANDA KOT *and* KUCHELA *(foreground), from below Unta Dhura (Harish Kapadia).*

26 NANDA KOT (6861 M)
This stunning mountain is the Fortress of the Goddess in the Nanda Devi legend. It was first attempted by T. Longstaff in 1905 from the Lwa valley, and he had to prevail with his experience upon his enthusiastic guides to abandon the climb. It was first climbed by a Japanese team (Y. Hotta) in 1936 and thereafter by the Indians in 1959. The Japanese celebrated the fiftieth year of its first ascent by repeating the climb in 1986.

27 SUDARSHAN PARBAT, *east face (Bernard Odier).*

28 VASUKI PARBAT *(Trevor Braham).*

27 SUDARSHAN PARBAT (6507 M)
A prominent mountain seen clearly from the Gangotri temple. First climbed by its east face in 1981 by an Indo-French team (Harish Kapadia), two Japanese ascents followed in 1984 and 1985, one of them by the southwest ridge. It is still an attractive challenge because of the ease of approach. According to legend Sudarshan is the chakra *in the hands of Krishna, to be used for ultimate destruction; when released, victory is certain.*

28 VASUKI PARBAT (6792 M)
Named after the shape of Vasuki, the famous king of snakes. It is imposing and was first climbed in 1973 by the I.T.B.P. (L. P. Semwell). Fifteen years passed before its second ascent in 1988 by the Italians (C. Marcello).

29 SHIVLING, *southeast face (Jerzy Wala).*

29 SHIVLING (6543 M)
A prominent peak in the Gangotri glacier, named after Shiva. A brief recce by the Austrians in 1938 was followed many years later by two Indian attempts in 1973 and 1974. The mountain was first climbed in 1974 by the I.T.B.P. (Hukam Singh) *by its west face, and within weeks another Indian team (L. P. Sharma) got to the top using the same route. The fine route up the steep east pillar was climbed by the British (Doug Scott) in 1981, while Shivling West (6501 m) was ascended by an equally elegant line in 1983 by Chris Bonington and Jim Fotheringham. Many variations have been executed since then and many more are possible on this symbol of Shiva's creative force.*

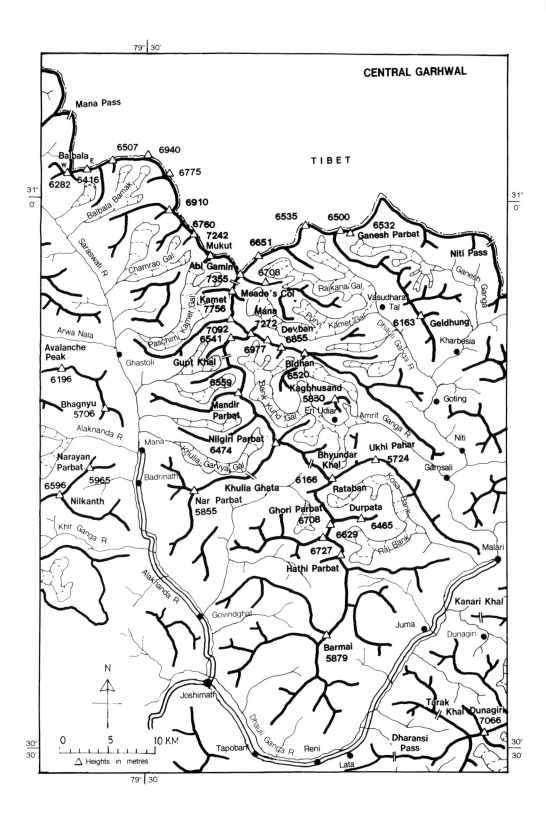

CENTRAL GARHWAL

TIBET

Mana Pass

Balbala E   6507   6940
        W   6775
6282   6416
                Balbala Bamak   6910
    Saraswati R.   6760
                Chamrao Gal.   7242
                                        Mukut   6535   6500   6532
                                                    6651   Ganesh Parbat   Niti Pass
                                    Abi Gamin   Ganesh Ganga
                                    7355   6708
Arwa Nala   Meade's Col   Raikana Gal.   Vasudhara
                        Kamet   Mana   Tal
                        7756   7272   Purv   Kamet Gal.   6163   Geldhung
Avalanche   7092   Devban   Dhauli Ganga R.   Kharbesia
Peak   Ghastoli   6541   6855
                                    6977   Bidhan
6196   Gupt Khal   6520
                                    6559   Kagbhusand   Goting
Bhagnyu   5830
5706   Mandir   Eri Udiar   Amrit Ganga R.   Niti
        Alaknanda R.   Parbat   Gamsali
Narayan   Mana   Nilgiri Parbat   Ukhi Pahar
Parbat   6474   Bhyundar   5724
6596   5965   Khulia Garvyal Gal.   Khal
        Nilkanth   Badrinath   6166   Rataban   Malari
                            Khulia Ghata   Durpata
Khir Ganga R.   Nar Parbat   Ghori Parbat   6465
                        5855   6708   6629
                                    6727   Raj Bank   Kanari Khal
                            Hathi Parbat
                    Govindghat   Juma   Dunagiri
        N   Tarak
                                    Barmai   Khal   Dunagiri
                                    5879   7066
    0   5   10 KM   Joshimath
    △ Heights in metres   Tapoban   Dhauli Ganga R.   Reni   Dharansi
                                            Lata   Pass

CENTRAL GARHWAL

CENTRAL GARHWAL comprises the mountain area around the Saraswati-Alaknanda river system and the Dhauli valley. The Dhauli after joining up with the Rishi Ganga (emerging from the protection of the Nanda Devi Sanctuary) eventually joins the Alaknanda at Joshimath.

The region is of some considerable significance in Hindu mythology, and Badrinath on the Alaknanda is one of the four holy places of pilgrimage – the others being Kedarnath, Jamnotri and Gangotri.

The very earliest travellers from the west were the Jesuits on their way to and from Tibet over the Mana pass. But the exploration and mapping started, as usual, with the survey parties from the Survey of India.

Kamet (7756 m), the prominent point of this area, was surveyed by R. Strachey in 1848 and the climbing attempts began soon after. The Schlagintweits came in 1855 and named the peaks Western, Central and Eastern Ibi Gamin, identifiable today as Mukut Parbat (7242 m), Kamet and Abi Gamin (7355 m). Mana (7272 m) was also visited. There was still some confusion in establishing the topography of this group, until I. S. Pocock set up his plane-table, and under the stewardship of E. C. Ryall of the Survey of India sorted matters out between the years 1874–77.[1]

W. W. Graham had an extremely active year in 1884. Having spent the spring in Sikkim, he arrived at Joshimath by 6 July, tried his hardest to force the Rishi gorge to climb Nanda Devi, attempted Dunagiri, but was beaten by bad weather, and finally claimed the ascent of Pk A21 (now known as Changabang) with no great difficulty! From his description of the mountain it was obvious that he was mistaken, and the guess is that he was on one of the smaller peaks on the southern or Hanuman ridge of Dunagiri.[2] Later in the year he returned to Sikkim, to make his claimed ascent of Kabru which was possibly Forked Peak. Sir Martin Conway was generous in his judgement during the debate on the Kabru ascent: 'Nothing is easier than to make a mistake in such a case.' To which Kenneth Mason adds the prediction that 'in the Himalaya, he would be neither the first nor the last to do so.' Prophetic words, except that in these days of reliable maps and detailed literature, one has no excuse to be as enthusiastically naive as Graham was in his days.

After his success on Trisul (7120 m) in 1907 (of which more later) Longstaff turned his attention to the Kamet area. But the route from the Purvi (East) Kamet glacier was raked by ice-avalanches and no safe passage could be discerned. They therefore explored some of the access from the west, before turning their attention elsewhere.

Between 1910 and 1914 C. F. Meade and Capt A. M. Slingsby put in some hard work on Kamet. Meade made an attempt in 1910. Slingsby approached it from the west the following year. Meade was there again in 1912 and reached a col, now known as the 'Slingsby Saddle', and then returned later in the year to try an approach from the Raikana valley. The next year he made a determined bid along the Purvi Kamet glacier and reached the col (named after him) between Kamet and Abi Gamin, and just missed the summit because of snow conditions. That year (1913) Slingsby made an equally strong bid from the west but was defeated by bad weather. Meade had certainly opened the route, but it was not until 1931[3] that Frank Smythe and his merry men (Shipton, Holdsworth, Greene and Birnie, with two Sherpas) made the first ascent, thus recording Kamet as the highest peak climbed to date. The second ascent was in 1954 by an Indian team led by Nandu Jayal, and in recent years it has been climbed quite often, the only novel variation being provided by the Indo-French expedition of 1986 (Col B. S. Sandhu)[4] who made an ascent by its formidable west ridge.

Kamet's neighbour Abi Gamin was first climbed in 1950 by a team comprising R. Dittert, K. Berril, A. Tissieres and G. Chevally, who approached from the north.[5] Since then, it has regularly been climbed from Meade's Col.

There were only a few expeditions to Central Garhwal before the 1950s – but the major ones did some excellent field work. The first to come was the indomitable Frank Smythe in 1937. He had already visited the Bhyundar valley

in 1931 (after the Kamet expedition) and had very appropriately named it The Valley of Flowers, a botanist's paradise. Unfortunately, recent depredations by trekkers and
climbers alike and the wholesale plucking of rare plants have
forced the authorities to restrict entry to this valley to single
day-trips only. Smythe climbed Nilgiri Parbat, Blue Mountain (6474 m), and attempted Rataban, Red Arrow (6166
m). Crossing the Bhyundar in search of a route to Mana
(7272 m), he eventually made its first ascent, climbing up
from Gupt Khal and over a high point to its summit. On this
trip he also climbed Devban (Deoban on old maps) (6855
m) and Pk 6520 m, which has been unofficially christened
'Bidhan Parbat' by a successful Bengali team in 1968.[6]
Being a personalised name in memory of Sir Bidhan
Chandra Roy, former Chief Minister of Bengal, it is not
likely to become official but has gained some currency in the
meantime. Smythe's book of this expedition has of course
become a classic.[7] Next to follow was the Swiss team with
Andre Roch in 1939 who first attempted Chaukhamba
(7138 m), approaching it from its north face and east ridge.
Unfortunately they lost two Sherpas in an avalanche.[8]
Chaukhamba was eventually climbed in 1952 by a French
team (V. Russenberger). Roch turned his attention to the
other bank of the Saraswati and climbed Ghori Parbat,
Horse Peak (6708 m), followed by Rataban (6166 m), both
first ascents. A whole host of lesser summits were also
ascended.

In 1947 Roch was back[9] with his countrymen when they
achieved a first ascent of Balbala (6416 m) from the Jagrao
glacier. The summit team comprised R. Dittert, A. Graven,
A. Lohner, A. Roch, A. Sutter and Sherpas Wangdi Norbu
and Tenzing – the last named going from strength to
strength until his fine achievement on Everest in 1953 (after
which he became known as Tenzing Norgay). In the same
year Trevor Braham crossed over from the Kalindi Khal
into this region. He traversed the Bhyundar Khal, climbing
peaks and exploring the area.[10]

In 1950, a Scottish team under W. H. Murray[11] crossed
the Girthi gorge, a tributary of the Dhauli. They trekked in
the Siraunch valley and crossed the Unta Dhura (pass) into

Kumaon. Apart from climbing some unnamed peaks in the northern rim of the Nanda Devi Sanctuary, they made the first ascent of Uja Tirche (6202 m) and attempted Lampak (6325 m). An extremely well travelled expedition.

With this expedition the first phase of exploratory climbing was over; the second phase is still in progress where the smaller valleys with challenging peaks of modest height wait to be visited. Meanwhile some of the major ascents in this area have been those of Mukut Parbat (7242 m) by New Zealanders in 1951,[12] Hathi Parbat (6727 m) in 1963 by an I.T.B.P. team and Ganesh Parbat (6532 m) in 1965 by the Indian Police.[13] Smythe's 1937 route on Mana was repeated by an Indo-U.S. Armies team (Maj Chavan) in 1988, and in the same year the I.T.B.P. (Harbhajan Singh) climbed it from the Purvi Kamet glacier via the east face and the northeast ridge. But plenty remains for the mountaineer and explorer alike. Some tempting problems awaiting solutions are on Chalab (6160 m), Kholi (6114 m), Tirsuli West (7335 m), Mana Northwest (7092 m) and Lampak (6325 m), to name just a fraction of them.

A word or two on a small selection of peaks to the west of the Saraswati-Alaknanda divide – peaks that can be reached from Badrinath on the main road. There are two summits named Avalanche Peak (so called for the obvious reason). The first one lies on the Bhagnyu glacier (Pk 6196 m) and its avalanche caught early visitors T. H. Tilly and John Jackson in 1952. Jackson got off with light bruises, while poor Tilly ended up with a twisted knee and torn ligaments, and had to be carried back to base.[14] However Jackson returned with D. Bryson and climbed to the summit. The peak has been climbed since then without further mishaps. The second Avalanche Peak (6443 m) has an earlier history when Smythe and Shipton with two Sherpas were caught on it, in 1931, by not one but two avalanches. Smythe suffered a fractured rib and both were lucky to have got off alive. This summit lies to the south of Kalindi Khal which separates the Chaturangi glacier from the Arwa valley.

Mention must also be made of 'the Queen of the Garhwal', Nilkanth (6596 m), described as the second most beautiful mountain in the Himalaya after Siniolchu in

Sikkim. It is prominent from Badrinath itself – a sight that is lovely or awesome depending on whether one intends merely to sit back and admire or to climb it. It is a holy mountain, and presides over Badrinath from where it is worshipped by millions. Its south face is untouched, rising above the Panpatia glacier, and outside the Inner Line.

Unfortunately the claim of its first ascent in 1961[15] was smeared with the most unholy controversy which hardly reflected any credit on the climbing team, its leader or their sponsors. It was obvious from the beginning that the team was incapable of reading a map – all the heights of camps and prominent features were wrong in their first account. On closer scrutiny, the position of camps and timings of climbs had been changed to make the ascent sound more plausible; when queried they were changed once more. Even the shape of the summit underwent a metamorphosis. By now, too much of the reputation of the team leader and the sponsoring committee (a quasi-government body at the time) was at stake. Jagdish Nanavati, who almost single-handed fought for the truth by his careful and scientific arguments through a photo-chart and its orientation with the map contours, stood vindicated in the eyes of the mountaineering cognoscenti. But the cover-up and conclusions of the enquiry left a stale taste in the mouth.

CENTRAL GARHWAL REFERENCES
1 *Abode of Snow*, Kenneth Mason, p.82, London, 1955.
2 *Ibid.* pp.93–4.
3 *H.J.* Vol.IV, p.27 and *Kamet Conquered*, Frank Smythe, London, 1932.
4 *H.J.* Vol.43, p.42.
5 *H.J.* Vol.XVII, p.80.
6 *H.J.* Vol.XXVIII, p.89.
7 *The Valley of Flowers*, Frank Smythe, London, 1938.
8 *H.J.* Vol.XII, p.30.
9 *H.J.* Vol.XV, p.37.
10 *Ibid.* p.90.
11 *H.J.* Vol.XVI, p.38.
12 *H.J.* Vol.XVII, p.42.
13 *H.J.* Vol.XXVI, p.113.
14 *H.J.* Vol.XVIII, p.103.
15 *H.J.* Vol.41, p.122; *Nilkantha – Still Unclimbed?*, J. C. Nanavati, typescript in private circulation; *H.J.* Vol.XXIII, p.193; *Alpine Journal*, Vol.68, No.306, p.139; *H.J.* Vol.XXIV, p.148; *Alpine Journal*, Vol.69, No.308, p.145.

30 CHANGABANG, *north face and the Bagini pass*
(S. N. Dhar).

31 *Left,* KHOLI *and, right,* CHALAB, *from the Girthi glacier (west) (Arun Samant).*

32 NANDA GOND *from north of Unta Dhura (Harish Kapadia).*

33 KAGBHUSAND *from the Bank Kund valley (Harish Kapadia).*

Devban plateau. In 1931, on return from the ascent of Kamet, Shipton and Holdsworth got within 300 ft of the summit. Next day, Shipton paired with Nima Sherpa to make the first ascent, climbing 5200 ft that day. The only other ascent is reported by the I.T.B.P. in 1970.

34 RATABAN (6166 M)
The Red Arrow of the Gods stands over Bhyundar Khal. It was attempted by Frank Smythe in 1937 by its northwest face; the first ascent was made by the Swiss expedition of 1939 (A. Roch) by its south face. A British expedition (R. D. Greenwood) climbed the southeast face in 1951 and an Indo-New Zealand team (Col B. S. Sandhu) ascended in 1979.

35 NILKANTH (6596 M)
A peak towering above Badrinath temple. From 1937–61, it was attempted by various teams and different routes. An Indian team (Capt N. Kumar) claimed an ascent which was disproved upon scrutiny (though officially accepted by the I.M.F.). The first ascent was made by an I.T.B.P. team (S. P. Chamoli) but no details are available. The south face, above the Panpatia valley (open to travellers) is one of the major challenges left on this mountain named after Shiva.

34 RATABAN *from the Bank Kund valley (Harish Kapadia).*

30 BAGINI PASS (c.5800 M) *and* CHANGABANG (6864 M)
Changabang is a well known peak but its north face, seen here above the Bagini pass, is a most inviting challenge. The first ascent was made in 1974 by an Indo-British team (Chris Bonington) who climbed the east ridge. Subsequently, the peak has been climbed by its southwest face, the southeast face, its west wall and the south buttress.

31 CHALAB (6160 M) *and* KHOLI (6114 M)
Situated on the northeasterly extension of the Hardeol-Tirsuli ridge, Chalab has been attempted only once, by an Indian team which approached from the Girthi (west) glacier in 1988. They managed to overcome the icefall but were defeated by technical difficulties. Kholi is, as yet, unattempted. Both peaks are also formidable from the Milam glacier.

32 NANDA GOND (6315 M)
This inviolate peak is one of the northernmost peaks of the Nanda Devi legend and is therefore aptly known as the Veil of Nanda. It rises above the Unta Dhura, a pass above Milam on the famous trade route to Tibet.

33 KAGBHUSAND (5830 M)
A peak above the Amrit Ganga valley guarding the

35 NILKANTH, *south face, from Panpatia Bank (Jagdish Nanavati)*.

36 MANA, *west face, from Gupt Khal (Harish Kapadia).*

37 PURBI DUNAGIRI *from Bagini Bank (S. N. Dhar).*

38 CHIRBAS PARBAT *from the Jadh Ganga valley (Romesh Bhattacharjee).*

39 BANDARPUNCH WEST *(White Peak) from the Bandarpunch glacier (Harish Kapadia).*

36 MANA (7272 M)
Mana is situated on the divide of the Bank Kund and Purvi Kamet glaciers. This peak was first climbed by Frank Smythe who crossed the Bank Kund glacier and then climbed over the Gupt Khal (Secret Pass), so named because it is hidden until one is very close to it. The route then led over Pk 6541 m to the west-southwest of Mana, descending to the foot of the south ridge which was then followed to the summit. This was a remarkable route for a two-man team; even more so for the fact that it was done solo for most of the final climb. Mana resisted

two attempts, in 1961 and 1962, before permitting a second ascent in 1966. This was made by an Indian team which approached from the north. An Indian attempt in 1983 from the Gupt Khal proved unsuccessful, as did another, this time via the northeast face in 1985. In 1988 the east face was climbed by the I.T.B.P. (H. Singh), and the west face by the Indo-U.S. Army team (Maj Chavan), the latter following Smythe's route of 1937. A number of challenging routes still remain on this massif.

37 PURBI DUNAGIRI (6489 M)
A neighbour of the famous Dunagiri. The obvious approach is from the Bagini Bank, to its north. It was attempted in 1987, and finally climbed by two members of an Indian team (S. K. Ghosh) in 1988, when both summitters fell to their deaths during descent. Its steep spires should give ideas to those fond of technical climbing.

38 CHIRBAS PARBAT (6529 M)
This remotely situated peak was climbed in 1986 by an Indian team (I. Mukherjee).

40 *Left,* SWETVARN *and, right,* SHYAMVARN *from the Swetvarn glacier (Harish Kapadia).*

39 BANDARPUNCH WEST (6102 M)
Previously known as White Peak, this southwesterly neighbour of Kalanag has a long approach of 18 km over the Bandarpunch glacier to its summit. It was first climbed in 1984 by an Indian team (Harish Kapadia) who followed its northeast ridge. The east face, that defied Gibson and Tenzing Norgay in 1950, remains unclimbed.

40 SHYAMVARN (6135 M) *and* SWETVARN (6340 M)
Two small but challenging peaks named after their respective glaciers, which lie off the Raktavarn glacier. They are named after their complexions – shyam *(black) and* swet *(white). Shyamvarn was climbed in 1985 by an Indian team (B. Nayak), while Swetvarn has resisted two attempts, in 1981 and 1984.*

41 CHATURBHUJ (6654 M) *and* YOGESHWAR (6678 M)
Four distinct ridges give the name to the first peak – chatur *(four),* bhuj *(hands). Yogeshwar is one of the names of Krishna. Both peaks are on the Jadh Ganga-Raktavarn divide. In 1981 the Indo-French expedition (Harish Kapadia) climbed Chaturbhuj, but failed on Yogeshwar. Many difficult routes on these peaks await the technically strong climber.*

41 *Above,* CHATURBHUJ, *from Swetvarn Peak (Ramakant Mahadik). Below* YOGESHWAR *from Sudarshan Parbat (Bernard Odier).*

NANDA DEVI SANCTUARY

THE CENTRE-PIECE of the Garhwal region is, without doubt, the Nanda Devi Sanctuary. Until 1934 the gorge of the Rishiganga and the immediate area around Nanda Devi was the least known and most inaccessible part of the Himalaya. The mountain stands in a vast amphitheatre, seventy miles in circumference, and about 6000 m high. There is no depression in this cirque below 5200 m, except in the west where the Rishiganga, draining some 240 square miles of ice and snow, carves out for itself one of the most formidable gorges.

The early Indian Surveyors and mountaineers alike were unable to penetrate the fastness of the Inner Sanctuary. W. W. Graham made a start in 1883, after which famous mountaineers like Longstaff, Bruce, Ruttledge,[1] Wilson and Somervell all made attempts to force the gorge. It was left to Eric Shipton and Bill Tilman eventually to worm their way through to the Sanctuary in 1934,[2] preparing the way for an Anglo-American expedition in 1936 to make the ascent of Nanda Devi (7816 m)[3] when Tilman and Odell reached the top on 29 August – a height record that stood till the French climbed Annapurna in 1950.

What does the Inner and Outer Sanctuary comprise? The Inner Sanctum bears some similarity to a wrong-way round letter E (Ǝ) with the middle horizontal stroke made up of Nanda Devi main and east peaks. The other peaks which form on the other strokes of the letter comprise Latu Dhura (6392 m), Sakram (6254 m), Bamchu (6303 m), Deo Damla (6620 m), Mangraon (6568 m), Kalanka (6931 m) and Changabang (6864 m). Then after the Rishi opening, to its south, lie Maiktoli (6803 m), Devtoli (6788 m), Devistan (6678 m), Panwali Dwar (6663 m) and Nanda Khat (6611 m). Most of these can be approached from outside the Sanctuary. The outer bastion of the Sanctuary is easier to get into – indeed it has afforded rich grazing ground for shepherds for centuries. On the outer rim lie Ronti (6063 m), Nanda Ghunti (6309 m), Trisul (7120 m), Bethartoli Himal (6352 m), Hanuman (6075 m), Dunagiri (7066 m) and Mrigthuni (6855 m).

Imagine the fascination of the perilous Rishi gorge, and then, after a mini-mountain climb, to emerge finally into the peaceful valley of the upper Rishi – the goddess herself presiding over a panorama of indescribable beauty and peace. When Shipton and Tilman first broke through, there were herds of *bharal* totally unafraid at the approach of man. Alas, the love of mountain beauty was short-lived. In a few decades the Sanctuary resembled a combination of a garbage dump and a badly maintained public toilet, the animal life reduced to intruding man, the juniper and undergrowth mercilessly destroyed to provide firewood. The Sanctuary is now a National Park, which officially disallows anyone to enter it.

Almost immediately after the first ascent of Nanda Devi in 1936 a party of surveyors under Osmaston, and guided by Shipton himself, entered the Sanctuary and carried out the first reliable survey of this hitherto unknown area.[4] Shipton and Tilman had done some creditable plane-tabling, but now an authoritative map was in the making.

The second ascent of Nanda Devi in 1951 comprised a bold plan to climb the main peak and traverse from the main to the east summit along the connecting ridge. It was the French expedition led by Roger Duplat.[5] Duplat and Vignes were last seen close to the summit going strongly and it is presumed that they reached the top. They were not seen again. Meanwhile, as per plan, the support part established a camp on Longstaff Col, and three more towards the summit of Nanda Devi East. When there was no sign of the main climbers, Dubost and Tenzing Norgay climbed to the east summit in fierce winds, making its second ascent, but here, too, there was no sign of Duplat and Vignes, and the expedition reluctantly withdrew.

The east peak (7434 m) had received its first ascent in 1939 by a Polish team led by M. A. Karpinski, who approached it from the east via Lwa Gad, Naspanpatti and up Longstaff Col,[6] finally taking the same route that was followed by the French.

The traverse of the main and east peaks was the aim of the Indo-French expedition led by Y. Pollet Villard in 1975.[7] The two peaks were climbed on the same day – 16 June, but the plan for each summit party to traverse to an intermediate bivouac and continue the other side was given up in the face of the oncoming monsoon.

The elusive traverse was finally achieved in 1976[8] by an Indo-Japanese team jointly led by K. Kano and Jagjit Singh. After ascending the east summit, a camp E-4 was placed on the ridge just below the summit. Simultaneously on reaching the main summit, a camp W-5 was placed on the connecting ridge. Hasegawa and Takami (the east peak summitters) traversed towards the main summit and reached W-5 where Kato and Teramoto (the main peak summitters) awaited them. A day was lost in that camp due to a snowstorm, the east summit pair climbed to the main summit and descended by the well supported south ridge. A magnificent effort carefully planned and brilliantly executed.

1976 also saw the fortieth anniversary expedition jointly led by Ad Carter (who was a member of the team for the first ascent in 1936) and Willi Unsoeld, and sponsored by the A.A.C. and the I.M.F. The aim was to celebrate the occasion by a new and difficult route and the northwest ridge and the north buttress was selected.[9] Some brilliant climbing by Roskelley, States and Reichardt brought them success on a route scoured by avalanches and every kind of technical difficulty. Alas, Nanda Devi Unsoeld, Willi's daughter and the prime mover of the idea, was in the last camp awaiting her turn to try for the summit, when all the neglected illness (hiatus hernia, chronic dysentery complicated by anorexia) hit her and before she could be evacuated, suddenly collapsed and died in her father's arms. A chastened party returned to base.

Some of the other variations on Nanda Devi comprise the north ridge and the west face. The former was tried by a Czech team led by V. Starcala and V. Smida in 1978[10] when they were able to reach a high point (a subsidiary peak) on the ridge (Pk 6895 m), but further progress was abandoned due to foul weather after having reached another high point, on the way to the main summit. Several other ascents and attempts have been made but, not unwisely, the powers-that-be at last took note of the ecological devastation the annual rush of expeditions causes, and for the time being the Sanctuary is closed to all visitors.

Let us go around the Sanctuary Wall and describe some of the climbing on the peaks that are situated on it. Latu Dhura (6392 m) seems to have been left alone. At least there are no records of expeditions on it. Sakram (6254 m)[11] has been recently climbed by a British team led by Colin Read who also climbed Changabang – a fine ascent of its southeast face in 1976. Both Sakram in 1934 and Deo Damla (6620 m) in 1936 were climbed by Shipton's party. Bamchu (6303 m), Rishi Pahar (6992 m) and Pk 6911 m (christened 'Saf Minal') on the Uttar Rishi glacier were first ascents by an energetic Japanese team led by K. Shimizu in 1975.[12] Mangraon (6568 m) has had little attention, but Kalanka (6931 m) and Changabang (6864 m) have had several ascents, the latter by some spectacular routes. Its first ascent was by an Indo-British team jointly led by Chris Bonington and Balwant Sandhu in 1974.[13] The route lay over 'Shipton's Col' dividing Ramani from the Changabang glacier and to the saddle between the peak and Kalanka, thence by its east ridge. The spell of invincibility was broken. Subsequent ascents took on the more fearsome aspects of the mountain. Success was attained in 1976 by the southwest face by the Japanese (M. Toda), by the southeast face by the British (Colin Read) and by its sheer west wall by the great Boardman-Tasker combination – a real tour de force which capped a remarkable year for the mountain. Its formidable south buttress was yet another brilliant route pioneered by the Anglo-Polish team (V. Kurtyka) in 1978,[14] and repeated by the Italians (R. Lingua) in 1981[15] and by the Australians (C. Nottle) in 1982. Meanwhile another Australian party had approached from the Changabang glacier and after gaining the col between Changabang and Kalanka, summitted presumably by the route of the first ascent. Where will an ascent of a new route come from next? The north face still awaits a visitor.

Kalanka (6931 m), though quite overshadowed in popularity by its more spectacular neighbour, has also kept its interests alive. The first ascent was by a Japanese team led by I. Tanabe in 1975.[16] In 1977 the Czechs led by F. Grant climbed from the north.[17] They first attempted a *diretissima* up the 80° granite north face. Beaten by the weather, they tried the saddle between Kalanka and Changabang (from the north it is a formidable prospect) and followed the normal ridge to the top. The following year a British pair, R. D. Barton and A. F. Fyffe, got to the top via the south-east flank.[18] It seems that the northern aspects of both these peaks are the challenges for the future.

Dunagiri (7066 m) lies across the Ramani glacier from Changabang. It was attempted in 1883 by W. W. Graham; Longstaff had a look at it and considered the southwest ridge as a possible route. P. R. Oliver with D. Campbell made a serious attempt on it in 1933[19] from the west, as Longstaff had advised, but once having reached a plateau-like feature, they found themselves cut off from the rest of the ridge by a sharp knife-edge climb of 1200 m at an average angle of 50° with no possible site for a tent. That was that, and they turned their attention to Trisul which they climbed. As a member of Major Osmaston's survey party to the Nanda Devi region in 1936, Eric Shipton also had an opportunity to make an attempt on Dunagiri,[20] again from the southwest, and was faced with similar problems of access as Oliver. The peak was again attempted in 1937 by F. Smythe and Oliver, but it was the Swiss (Andre Roch) in 1939[21] who made the first ascent from the same saddle on the southwestern ridge previously occupied by Graham and Oliver, and then up the formidably long west ridge to the top. The modern style of the 'hard way up' could not have been better demonstrated than by Joe Tasker and Dick Renshaw when they climbed (second ascent) the south rib on the southeast face alpine-style in six days, 3–8 October, 1975[22] – a fantastic performance by any standard. Expeditions that have followed have been singularly prone to accident. Americans Brad Shaver and Karl Kerton, having reached the summit, fell to their deaths in bad weather in October, 1978.[23] Earlier, in 1976, four Americans fell to their deaths. The peak has been regularly climbed since then, by the Japanese, Australians, Poles and the Spaniards.

On the south side of the Rishi gorge lies Bethartoli Himal (6352 m), first attempted by W. H. Murray with the Scottish expedition in 1950.[24] Its southern outlier (Bethartoli South, 6318 m) was climbed in 1956 by Fritz Hieber and Sherpa Gyalzen, who descended to the col between the south and main peaks, but lack of time stopped further progress. That the mountain's approaches are guarded by objective dangers was demonstrated by the tragedy that befell a Bombay team (Prof R. Desai) in 1970.[25] After the ascent of Bethartoli South up the east face, the party concentrated their efforts on the main peak, but fate decreed otherwise. An able-bodied party comprising Ang Kami (Everester, 1965), Chawang Phinzo, Sherpa Gnappa, Passang Temba, Pemba Tchering, Arun Samant and Nitin Patel were retreating from C3 in the face of a continuous and fierce blizzard, when they were enveloped in an avalanche descending from the south face of the east ridge. The first three were buried without a trace. Nitin was found dead and was subsequently buried after the storm had abated. Arun, with Passang Temba staggered back to C1 where they were attended and rescue operations organised. The south peak was climbed again by the Americans in 1977; the main peak was finally climbed the same year by the Italians (Renato Moro) who, having noted the avalanche-prone slopes of the south-eastern aspects, chose to approach along the north ridge which they attained from the basin below the northeast face. The ridge to the summit was in parts heavily corniced, knife-edged and rotten rock along the way. Four members made the first ascent on 17 September.

Trisul (7120 m), of course, has a much earlier history, having had its first ascent as far back as 1907 by Longstaff with the two Swiss guides, the Brocherel brothers, and Karbir, his Gurkha assistant. At the time it stood as a height record. Being a relatively easy mountain (by its normal route) it has been climbed innumerable times. In 1978 the Japanese (S. Inada)[26] led a two-pronged ascent of Trisul I and II (6690 m) from the south ridge of the main peak (north ridge of Trisul II), a new approach route altogether. Earlier, in 1960, the Yugoslavs (Ales Kunaver) had climbed Trisul II and III (6008 m)[27] from the Bidalgwar glacier to the south of the Sanctuary Wall. In 1987 they were back (V. Lado)[28] and climbed the main peak from the unclimbed west face, then proceeded to split the summit party, two of them para-jumping 3000 m to the camp below, and the others completing a traverse of Trisul II and III. Vlasta Kunaver, the daughter of Ales who led the 1960 expedition, was one of the para-jumpers. Trisul now patiently awaits the hang-gliders!

Mrigthuni (6855 m), lying at the head of Trisul nala, received its first ascent in 1958[29] when Aamir Ali, Gurdial Singh, Rajendra Singh, along with the Garhwalis Kalyan Singh and Dewan Singh, approached the south face and clambered onto the east ridge just before the summit (19 June, 1958). Thereafter it has had several ascents.

Devistan (6678 m) was climbed by Hari Dang's party in 1961, having retreated from their attempt on Nanda Devi.[30] They also climbed Maiktoli (6803 m) and Trisul – two ascents, one of them by climbing all night in moonlight and summitting at dawn.

Devistan II (6529 m) was also climbed during an Indian Nanda Devi expedition (Capt N. Kumar) in 1964, when B. P. Singh with a Sherpa and two porters climbed up and descended on the same day (24 June, 1964). They also achieved their main objective, Nanda Devi (Nawang Gombu and Dawa Norbu on 20 June, 1964).

Devtoli (6788 m) lies on the ridge between Devistan and Maiktoli, hence the combination name accorded to it by Harish Kapadia who led its first ascent in 1974, with a team from Bombay.[31] The approach was from the South Rishi glacier and up a col between the peak and Maiktoli, thence to the summit. The price of success was a broken leg for the leader who fell into a crevasse when a snow bridge collapsed during the descent; rather than hang himself by the tightening strands of the belay rope, he cut himself loose, fell a further forty feet to the bottom and sustained the injury. The rescue, from 20,000 ft to 13,800 ft to base, was painfully carried out in thirteen days and finally a helicopter lifted him out of his misery to proper medical attention.

On the periphery of the Sanctuary stand the two peaks of Ronti (6063 m) and Nanda Ghunti (6309 m). The first ascent of Ronti was by Peter Aufschnaiter and George Hampson in 1955.[32] The second ascent in 1967 was by a

ladies' team (Miss Deepali Sinha).[33] Nanda Ghunti's first
ascent was one of several climbs made by the Swiss expeditions of 1947.[34] Approaching by the Nandakini valley, Roch
and Dittert made their ascent over a col, and the east ridge,
which is a far from easy proposition. Since then quite a few
ascents have been recorded.

NANDA DEVI SANCTUARY REFERENCES

1 *H.J.* Vol.V, p.28.
2 *H.J.* Vol.VII, p.1.
3 *H.J.* Vol.IX, p.21.
4 *Ibid.* p.74.
5 *H.J.* Vol.XVII, p.60 and *To Kiss High Heaven*,
   J. J. Languepin, London, 1956.
6 *H.J.* Vol.XII, p.65.
7 *H.J.* Vol.XXXIV, p.59.
8 *H.C.N.L.* 32, p.10.
9 *H.J.* Vol.XXXV, p.186.
10 *H.J.* Vol.36, p.189.
11 *H.C.N.L.* 32, p.12.
12 *H.J.* Vol.XXXIV, p.53.
13 *H.J.* Vol.XXXIII, p.88.
14 *H.C.N.L.* 33, p.2.
15 *H.J.* Vol.38, photo facing p.165;
   also *H.C.N.L.* 35, p.22.
16 *H.C.N.L.* 32, p.3.
17 *H.J.* Vol.XXXV, p.294.
18 *H.C.N.L.* 34, p.1.
19 *H.J.* Vol.VI, p.91.
20 *H.J.* Vol.IX, p.74.
21 *H.J.* Vol.XII, p.30.
22 *H.J.* Vol.XXXIV, p.155.
23 *H.J.* Vol.36, p.192.
24 *H.J.* Vol.XVI, p.38.
25 *H.J.* Vol.XXX, p.188.
26 *H.J.* Vol.36, p.58.
27 *H.J.* Vol.XXII, p.70.
28 *H.C.N.L.* 41, p.37.
29 *H.J.* Vol.XXI, p.86.
30 *H.J.* Vol.XXV, p.95.
31 *H.J.* Vol.XXXIII, p.104.
32 *H.J.* Vol.XX, p.125.
33 *H.C.N.L.* 25, p.4.
34 *H.J.* Vol.XV, p.39.

42 LAMPAK I *from the Siraunch valley (A. C. Shelat).*

43 SHILLA, *east face (Harish Kapadia).*

42 LAMPAK I (6325 M)
The Lampak group, rising above the Siraunch valley, was first noticed by the Scottish Himalaya expedition in 1950 (W. H. Murray). The only reported ascent was in 1969 by an Indian party (P. Chakraborty), by its southwest buttress.

43 SHILLA (6132 M)
In 1860, a khalasi of the Survey of India climbed this remote peak. It remained as an altitude record for forty-seven years, as the height was computed to be 23,064 ft. However, modern survey has diminished it to 20,120 ft (6132 m). But by then a place had already been

secured in history for this Place of the Monastery. It is very remote, difficult to approach, and has only recently been photographed from close quarters.

44 GYAGAR (6400 M)
A beautiful high peak between the Lingti and Chaksachan nalas in Spiti,

44 GYAGAR, *west face (Harish Kapadia).*

45 CENTRAL PEAK *in the Bara Shigri glacier (Peter Holmes).*

it defeated an attempt in 1987 and remains unclimbed. Its name means Indian. It is strategically located and can be seen prominently from Tibet (Pare Chu).

45 CENTRAL PEAK (6285 M)
This mountain rises at the northeast end of Bara Shigri, amidst a veritable jungle of peaks. It was first climbed by two British women and two Sherpas in 1961 (J. Scarr). They reached the saddle between Central Peak and its southern neighbour, Lion (6126 m), and then climbed both peaks. These peaks have had repeated ascents thereafter.

46 JORKANDEN *from Kalpa (Harish Kapadia).*

46 JORKANDEN (6473 M)
The highest peak in the Kinner-Kailash range; one can admire it comfortably from a bungalow at Kalpa. Often mistaken and called Kinner Kailash (which is a smaller holy pillar to the north of it). It has been climbed by the I.T.B.P. in 1974, and by the Indian Para Regiment in 1978.

47 GYA (6794 M)
The highest peak in Himachal Pradesh remained unknown till the late 1980s. This stupendous rock monolith at the tri-junction of Spiti (Lingti valley), Ladakh (Rupshu) and Tibet (Pare Chu) offers a long and difficult approach to the base of one of the finest rock-climbing challenges still left.

47 GYA *from the Gyagar ridge (Harish Kapadia).*

GANGOTRI REGION

WE NOW CROSS the Alaknanda-Saraswati divide and move westwards to the mighty Gangotri complex. The early maps were fairly vague and misleading and it was not until the 1936 surveys under Maj Gordon Osmaston[1] were carried out, covering ground from the Satluj watershed in the west to the borders of Nepal in the east, that some semblance of order was imposed as far as authenticity of heights and positions was concerned. Some heroic tales can be recounted of the surveyors braving blizzards and being snowbound for days, to be rescued along with their *khalasis* in the last stages of survival, but still clutching their precious plane-table survey – Fazl Elahi was one such.

The major glaciers that describe the Gangotri region are the Gangotri, Chaturangi and Raktavarn, which lie adjacent to each other. Separated from them by massive walls of peaks lie the Satopanth, Bhagirathi and the Arwa valley. Each of them has feeder glaciers, and each feeder glacier has numerous peaks along its walls. A glance at the map shows the enormity of the problem of description. The following account can only be a selection of the major climbing achievements. We enter the area by the Bhagirathi river – Gangotri is the last settlement, and the roadhead. At Gaumukh (Cow's Mouth), one observes the mighty river, the source of the holy Ganges, emerging from the depths of the glacier, and the shape of the ice formation is indeed like a cow's mouth.

Immediately opposite is Shivling (6543 m), a towering pinnacle of rare beauty – and of equally severe technical difficulty. It was only after the latest developments in artificial climbing that serious attempts were made on this mountain. Its first ascent by the I.T.B.P. (Hukam Singh) in 1974 however preferred to dispense with style and elegance and reached the top after fixing 2100 m of fixed rope and peppering the west ridge with pitons (3 June);[2] the second ascent was seventeen days later when the instructors from the Nehru Institute of Mountaineering led by the Principal, Col L. P. Sharma, repeated the same route. In 1980 the

Japanese made the ascent from the west ridge and then a traverse under the summit snowfield to the north ridge and thence to the summit. In 1981 an Indo-British team (Doug Scott)[3] climbed to the summit via its east pillar – 1200 m in sixty rope-lengths over extremely exposed ridges. It took them thirteen days to achieve this. They descended by the north side. Style and elegance were displayed in full measure by Bonington and Fotheringham when in 1983 they made the first ascent of the west summit (6038 m) by its southeast ridge in a seven-day push.[4] Since then both the summits have been visited.

To the east of Gaumukh lies the Manda-Bhrigupanth massif. The Manda peaks are numbered north to south I–III. Thus Manda II is the highest followed by III and I. Manda I (6510 m) has not been a very popular mountain in spite of its proximity to Gangotri. It was reportedly climbed in 1978 by a team from Bengal but no details have come to hand.[5] A team from Bombay climbing from the Kedar Ganga side reached the summit in 1981[6] and it was subsequently climbed by the Japanese in 1982 by its north ridge; they also approached their goal from the Kedar Ganga valley. Manda II (6568 m), lying south of Manda I, was ascended in 1982 by P. Udall, P. Athans and P. O'Neil climbing to a col between Manda II and III (6529 m) and thence by its south ridge.

Bhrigupanth (6772 m) can be approached either from the west (Kedar Bamak) or from the east (Bhrigupanth Bamak). The first ascent was made in 1980 by a ladies' expedition of mixed nationalities.[7] They chose the western approach to a col between the peak and Thalay Sagar (6904 m) and then by the south ridge to the top. Again, it is an inexplicably little visited summit, whereas Jogin I (6465 m), II (6342 m) and III (6116 m) lying across the Kedar Bamak, have been more popular with Indians and foreigners alike. The British Police team in 1986[8] had a healthy respect for the mountains as well as a sense of humour. During the approach, they wore T-shirts reading 'We're going Jogin'. On the way out they changed into fresh ones which informed the public 'We've been Jogin'. In between, they had climbed Jogin I and III, attempted Manda III and climbed two minor summits in the area. Earlier, in 1971, a team from Jadavpur University (Amit Chowdhury)[9] climbed all three summits. Aided by good weather and cautious route-finding they made a competent sweep of the massif.

Thalay Sagar (6904 m) is a fantastic peak by any standards. Its first ascent was made by R. Kliegfield, J. Waterman, J. Thakray and P. Thexton in 1979,[10] by the northwest couloir and ridge. But a magnificent route was selected on its northeast pillar by the Polish-Norwegian expedition in 1983.[11] The route actually begins at the col separating the peak from Bhrigupanth (to its north), and some excellent granite, overhanging in parts, along with some mixed terrain, gave them a most satisfying summit. There are still some challenging routes to be found on this mountain.

Proceeding southwards along the Gangotri glacier one has the giant peaks of the Bhagirathi and Satopanth massif to one's east. At the head of the glacier at its far end lie the mighty Chaukhamba summits. On the western rim of the glacier we have the Kedarnath and Dome, Kharchakund, Sumeru Parbat and Mandani Parbat. Several unnamed peaks dot the peripheral walls of the glacier.

The Bhagirathi peaks I (6856 m), II (6512 m) and III (6454 m) lie fairly close to the junction of Raktavarn and Gangotri glaciers. Bhagirathi II in fact overlooks both, and has been the easiest to approach. The first ascent of Bhagirathi II was made by an Austrian-German team (R. Schwarzgruber) in 1938[12] when considerable time was spent in surveying the climbing prospects in this region. In the process, they also climbed Chandra Parbat (6739 m) on the Chaturangi glacier, Mandani Parbat (6193 m), Swachhand (6721 m) and Sri Kailas (6932 m), all first ascents. Bhagirathi II has had several ascents since then, and is a bit of a favourite for expeditions with only a little time to spare.

Bhagirathi I was first climbed in 1980 by a Japanese team via its southeast ridge, who used about 2000 m of rope. A small team of four British friends made an alpine-style ascent in 1983[13] by its west ridge that gave them some excellent rock climbing on granite and some tricky snow climbing. Martin Moran, Charlie Heard and John Mothersele got to the summit – a fine effort of clean climbing without festooning the rock with rope and ironmongery. Alas, on the descent, Heard fell to his death when an anchor came off during an abseil.

Some excellent routes on Bhagirathi II and III have been made. On Bhagirathi III, for instance, Bob Barton and Allen Fyffe made a fine ascent of the southwest buttress in 1982,[14] (described by George Bettembourg as 'an El Cap with a Droites north face on top, at 6000 m') and a descent by the north ridge. It was one of the best ascents in Garhwal that year. This route has been repeated by a team from New Zealand, in 1988.

Opposite the Bhagirathi peaks across the Gangotri glacier lies Kedarnath (6940 m) and its neighbour Kedar Dome (6831 m). Kedarnath was first climbed by the Swiss Garhwal expedition of 1947,[15] the first attempt having been repulsed by an accident to Sherpa Wangdi Nurbu, a veteran of several expeditions. That he was brought down and was able to recover to full health is a tribute to the Sherpas and Sahibs alike. The Dome is a slightly easier proposition and one of the earlier ascents was that in 1967 by a team from Bengal which had a multi-disciplined party (studying glaciology, geology, botany and sociology). Since then the Dome has been a favourite target for climbers. A new route on the South Face of Kedarnath was opened up by a Japanese team (M. Hoshino) in 1981.[16] They failed due to execrable weather and shortage of time, but they showed what could be done in the way of route variation even on a popular mountain. The south face was eventually climbed by the Italians in 1988.

Kharchakund (6612 m) lies further down the Gangotri glacier from Kedarnath. It has fine lines of ascent, not all of them having been exhausted. First climbed in 1980 by the Japanese by the west ridge, it resisted the next attempt in 1982 by a Scottish team. The second ascent was by the northeast wall, by an Austrian team (E. Lindenthaler). It repulsed a British party in 1984 and a German team in 1986. The difficult west ridge was finally climbed by a British party (R. Beadle) who reached the summit after a five-and-a-half-day alpine-style ascent in 1987.

Satopanth (7075 m) lies at the end of the bend of the Gangotri glacier which turns east and northwards. Its massive shape can be seen from most vantage points for miles around. It was first climbed by the Swiss (A. Roch) in 1947 during their well documented Garhwal expedition.[17] The climb was actually made from the Chaturangi glacier, up Sundar Bamak, skirting below Vasuki Parbat and then via the northeast spur and the north face of the peak.' An unofficial ascent appears to have been made in 1981 (when the area was still closed to foreigners) by Leon Lehrer and another European, climbing alpine-style. When the peak became open to climbing, the Japanese (K. Toya) were the earliest to reach the summit in 1982, again by the north face. 1983 saw seven teams attempting the peak, five of which were successful. A seven-thousander amidst a sea of six-thousanders has its own attraction, but the massif is full of novel routes to get up. The northeast ridge has been attempted several times. The eighth ascent in May 1984 by an Austrian party was the first by a variation of the north face route. The south face originally attempted by the Polish climbers in 1983 and 1984, and by the Japanese in 1984 was first ascended by the Poles in 1986.

Chaukhamba I (7138 m) along with II (7068 m), III (6974 m) and IV (6854 m) form the south and east boundary wall of the Gangotri glacier. It is the highest point in the Gangotri region. It was first climbed in 1952 by a French team who approached it from the Bhagirathi Kharak. The second ascent was by an Indian team (Commodore S. N. Goyal) also from the Bhagirathi Kharak, then up the north face and northwest ridge.[18] The team also attempted Nilkanth, without success. Since then Chaukhamba I has been climbed three times by Indian expeditions, but Chaukhamba II, III and IV await first ascents by the superstars – the going indeed is tough.

The other major glacier, the Chaturangi, is equally well-endowed with climbing prospects. Immediately to the east of the Bhagirathi peaks lies the shapely Vasuki Parbat (6792 m). First climbed by the I.T.B.P. in 1973 (L. P. Semwell) (no details available), it had resisted all comers until 1988 when the Italians (C. Marcello) made the second ascent. It offers an exciting and technically difficult ascent to anyone bold enough to have a shot at it. Of the recent attempts, there has been one made in 1979[19] by a Welsh team and another in 1985 by the French by a variation up the northwest ridge.[20] The main problem here is of rotten rock that continuously scours the face and ridge alike.

East of Vasuki lies the less formidable Chandra Parbat (6739 m), still a beautiful summit for the climber with variations of route in mind. Its first ascent was by the Germans (Prof. R. Schwarzgruber) in 1938[21] who climbed it by its west ridge without much difficulty. The second ascent was by an Indian team (Pilot Officer Raju) in 1965, and since then has been climbed by the I.T.B.P. in 1974 and by the Diganta Club of Calcutta (P. Mazumdar) in 1984.[22] At the head of the Chaturangi glacier lies the Kalindi Khal, separating it from the Arwa valley. There have been several crossings of this pass that enables the traveller to switch over from the Gangotri region to the Saraswati-Alaknanda side, though not without some hard work.

The other major glacier system is the Raktavarn which offers the possibilities of peaks such as Sudarshan Parbat (6507 m), Yogeshwar (6678 m) and the southern approach to Sri Kailas (6932 m), amongst many other unnamed ones. Even before one hits the Raktavarn, a short distance away from the Gangotri village, one faces to one's left the cirque comprising Chirbas Parbat (6529 m), Chaturbhuj (6654 m), Matri (6721 m) and Thelu (6002 m).

Sudarshan had eluded an ascent until 1981, by an Indo-French expedition.[23] It is by no means an easy peak and, of the several previous attempts, a couple could be described as cases of wrong identification of the mountain. Chaturbhuj also received its first ascent by the same expedition which made the second ascent of Saife (6161 m), lying on the southeastern limb of Sudarshan. They attempted Yogeshwar and Swetvarn (6340 m) to the northwest of Sudarshan. Smaller summits in the area were also climbed.

The area is of interest, particularly because of its proximity to the roadhead and the infrequency of its invasion.

GANGOTRI REGION REFERENCES
1 *H.J.* Vol.XI, p.128.
2 *H.C.N.L.* 30, p.23.
3 *H.J.* Vol.38, p.74.
4 *H.J.* Vol.40, p.70.
5 *H.C.N.L.* 32, p.46
6 *H.J.* Vol.39, p.60; also attempt, p.55.
7 *H.J.* Vol.41, p.175.
8 *H.J.* Vol.43, p.45.
9 *H.J.* Vol.38, p.173.
10 *H.J.* Vol.37, p.70.
11 *H.C.N.L.* 37, p.25.
12 *H.J.* Vol.XI, p.140.
13 *H.J.* Vol.40, p.87.
14 *Ibid.* p.79.
15 *H.J.* Vol.XV, p.18.
16 *H.J.* Vol.39, p.51.
17 *H.J.* Vol.XV, p.33.
18 *H.J.* Vol.XXIII, p.100.
19 *H.J.* Vol.37, p.75.
20 *H.J.* Vol.42, p.176.
21 *H.J.* Vol.XI, p.140.
22 *H.J.* Vol.42, p.35.
23 *H.J.* Vol.38, p.84.

48 MANIMAHESH KAILASH *from below Chobu pass (Harish Kapadia).*

48 MANIMAHESH KAILASH (5655 M)
Every range in the Himalaya has its own Kailash. This one in Chamba is a most formidable challenge by its southern approaches. It rises above the Manimahesh lake and the Chobu pass. The only ascent was made in 1968 by an Indo-Japanese ladies' team (N. Pandya) by the easier northern approach.

49 PAPSURA (6451 M) *and*
50 DHARAMSURA (6446 M)
*A prominent peak on the
watershed dividing the Tos
and the Bara Shigri glaciers
in Lahul, Papsura is the
Peak of Evil. To its
southeast is Dharamsura
which is the Peak of Good.
Papsura was first climbed in
1967 by a British team
(R. G. Pettigrew) which
came over the Malana
glacier, crossed the Pass of
the Animals and the
Papsura glacier to climb the
western couloir of the south
face to the summit, despite
an accident to the first
summit team. The second
ascent was made by a*

*British team in 1977. They
climbed the south face for
about 300 m and then
followed the difficult
southwest ridge.
Several expeditions have
confused Dharamsura with
Papsura. Dharamsura
(previously known as White
Sail) was first climbed by a
British expedition in 1941
(J. O. M. Roberts). They
followed the East Tos
glacier, climbed over to the
col due south of the peak,
and then followed the south
ridge to the summit. This
route was repeated by a
British team in 1961
(R. G. Pettigrew). There
have been several other*

*ascents of this peak.
A peak of 5954 m on the
continuation of the
Papsura-Dharamsura ridge
has often been confused with
Dharamsura, thus creating
more confusion about
claims. The climbing
histories are now sorted out
and there is a lot more yet to
be written on this area.*

49 PAPSURA, *upper slopes (Z. Rangwala).*

50 DHARAMSURA, *northeast face (Aloke Surin).*

51 Z3 (6270 м) *from Pk 5557, Upper Durung Drung glacier, Zanskar (Geoff Cohen).*

51 Z3 (6270 м)
Originally known as Cima Italia, it lies on the periphery of the Durung Drung glacier; it was first climbed as far back as 1913 by an Italian party (M. Piacenza). The next ascent was sixty-eight years later, when G. Augustino led another Italian team in 1981. These ascents have been followed by yet another successful Italian attempt in 1982. A Japanese team also made an ascent in 1984.

52 GEPANG GOH
(5870 M)
*A fine, inviting peak above
the road to Keylang, first
climbed by Gen C. G.
Bruce. It has a group of
various summits and only a
few of these have been
climbed or attempted.*

52 GEPANG GOH *from the Rohthang pass
(Harish Kapadia).*

53 ASHAGIRI (*c.*6100 M)
*A peak above Kulti valley in
Lahul. The first ascent was
made in 1955 by a British
R.A.F. team (A. J. M.
Smythe) who gave it its
name.*

53 ASHAGIRI *from Kulti valley (J. R. Raul).*

54 PK 5990 M *Palphu, northeast area of Miyar nala, Lahul (Geoff Cohen).*

55 PHABRANG, *south face (Ramakant Mahadik).*   **56** MALANA TOWERS *(Colin Pritchard).*

54 PK 5990 M
*This peak lies in the Palphu
nala, off the Miyar valley in
Lahul. The area was
explored by Geoff Cohen
who made the first ascent in
1983, and also Pk 6020 m.
This subsidiary nala
contains a number of peaks
awaiting a second visit.*

55 PHABRANG (6172 M)
*This peak lying at the head
of the Karpat nala, a feeder
of the Miyar nala in Lahul,
was first climbed in 1972 by
a Japanese team (S.
Ibayashi). The most notable
venture on this peak has
been that of a British team
(D. V. Nicholls) in 1980.
They approached the
mountain by three routes
and were successful in*

57 BRAMMAH I *from Dhaula Dhar (Harish Kapadia).*

58 BRAMMAH II *(right) and* FLAT TOP *from southeast ridge of Brammah I (Chris Bonington).*

59 HAGSHU, *from the south (Stephen Venables).*

climbing the northwest face, the southwest face-south ridge combination route (over which the northwest face team descended), but were beaten on the north ridge and lost one member on the descent.

56 MALANA TOWERS (*c.*5500 M)
As the name suggests, this is a group of towers in the Malana valley near Manali. A few of these towers were climbed by a British team (Colin Pritchard) in 1966, with the Ladakhi Wangyal. Several so-called Manikaran Spires in the nearby Tos valley also await climbers.

57 BRAMMAH I (6416 M)

58 BRAMMAH II (6425 M) and FLAT TOP (6100 M)
Brammah I on the divide of the Kibar nala and the Nanth nala in Kishtwar was attempted twice by a British team (Dr Charles Clarke) in 1969 and 1971. In the latter attempt, they climbed the southeast ridge to within 100 m of the summit where they were beaten by poor snow conditions. An Indo-British team (Chris Bonington) made a fine first ascent by the southeast ridge in 1973 on their second attempt. A British team (Anthony Wheaton) repeated the same route in 1978 but lost two

members during the descent. A French team (S. Emanuel) climbed the north ridge in 1980. The neighbouring peaks of Brammah's Wife (5279 m), Flat Top (6100 m) and the nearby Brammah II (6425 m) combine to give this area a variety of difficult climbing. Brammah II was first climbed by a Japanese team (K. Keiro) in 1975 and Flat Top by a British team (Maj R. Wilson) in 1980.

59 HAGSHU (6300 M)
A peak rising above the Hagshu la. It has been attempted by British teams in 1985 (M. Rosser) and 1987 (S. Gascoyne).

60 KOLAHOI, *north face (John Hunt).*

60 KOLAHOI (5425 M)
The Kolahoi group of peaks arising above the Liddar valley in Kashmir have the dual advantages of easy access and variety of climbing, if height is not a consideration. It has been the scene of prolific climbing activity since the early years of this century. The first ascent of Kolahoi was made in 1912 from the north glacier, by 'the Neve-Mason couloir'. That famous pair of pioneers then followed the east ridge to the summit. A number of routes have been made on Kolahoi and surrounding peaks.

61 SASER KANGRI II (7518 M)
This broad topped peak in the Saser Musgtagh was first climbed by an Indo-Japanese team (H. Singh) in 1985. They chose to come over the Sakang Lungpa glacier from the Nubra side and climbed to the north ridge of Sakang (6750 m) and thereafter followed its continuation to the western summit of Saser Kangri II. The eastern summit (the same height) is separated by a plateau of about 1 km and remains unclimbed.

62 KANG YISSAY (6400 M)
This peak rising above the Nimaling plains in Zanskar has been a popular target in recent years; the north face and the southwest ridge offer a very good challenge with great possibilities. The normal route via the northwest ridge leads to Kang Yissay II.

61 SASER KANGRI II, *west peak (Masato Oki).*

62 *Southwest ridge of* KANG YISSAY *(Dhiren Pania).*

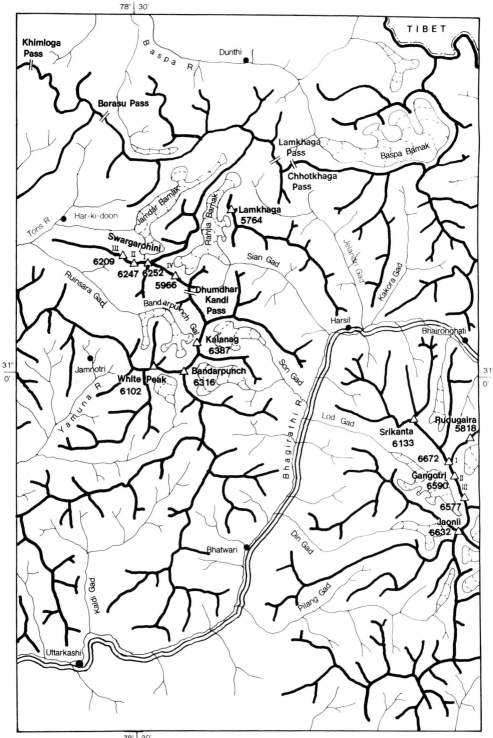

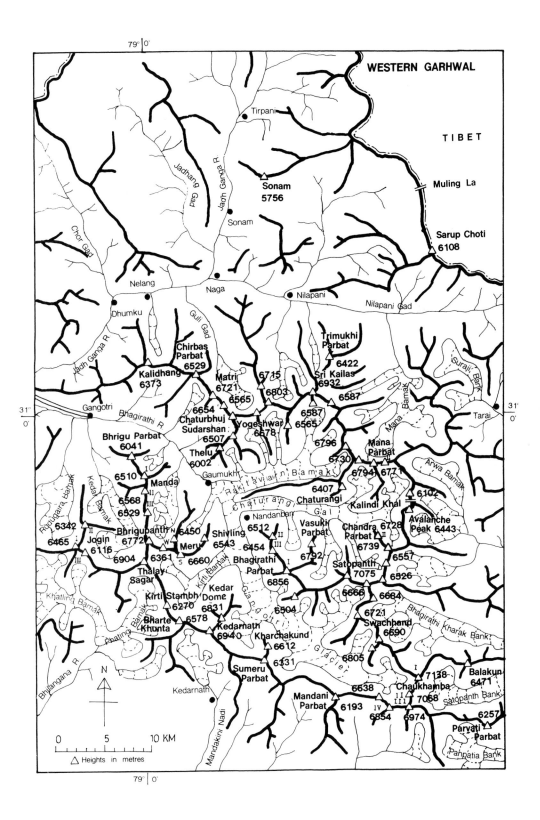

WESTERN GARHWAL

EST OF THE BHAGIRATHI, but more easily reached from Har-ki-doon and the Tons river, is a most attractive climbing arena comprising the Swargarohini (I–IV) and the Bandarpunch peaks – White Peak (6102 m), Bandarpunch (6316 m) and Kalanag (6387 m) (old Black Peak).

The area first came into prominence when the Doon School masters – R. L. Holdsworth, J. T. M. Gibson, J. A. K. Martyn and Gurdial Singh – used this area to offer climbing experience to their wards during summer holidays. In fact the first ascent of Bandarpunch in 1950 was by Jack Gibson and the young climbers. Since then the Nehru Institute of Mountaineering has taken its Advance Course students to the area and also climbed the peak in 1975.[1] Gibson and his boys also made the first ascent of Kalanag in 1955. The tradition was continued by Hari Dang (ex-pupil, now master in the Doon School) who led another summit party in 1968 to Kalanag, an excellent area for training youngsters to climb and ski.

Not so Swargarohini, all peaks of this massif being beyond the capabilities of beginners. Swargarohini II (6247 m) was climbed by the Canadians (Virk and Clarke) in 1974 and by a Bombay team (Anil Kumar) in 1985.[2] Two more Indian ascents were made when a Bombay party (R. Wadalkar) teamed up with an Oil and Natural Gas Commission expedition to reach the top.[3] Swargarohini III (6209 m) was also climbed (first ascent) by the 1985 Bombay party. Swargarohini I (6252 m) is an extremely tough proposition awaiting its first ascent.

It is an impossible task to convey comprehensively the tremendous wealth of climbing prospects in Garhwal. So many peaks remain unclimbed merely because they are unnamed and therefore of less publicity value. If ever someone just numbers the peaks with their heights (in the manner similar to Jerzy Wala's numerical depiction of the Hindu Kush), one will need to use five figures before the last one is awarded its place. The keen climber requires little imagination to stoke up his desire to visit Garhwal. He only needs to study the maps and borrow a few photographs from friends who have been there. The adrenalin flow should do the rest.

WESTERN GARHWAL REFERENCES
1 *H.J.* Vol.XXXIV, p.72.
2 *H.C.N.L.* 39, p.17.
3 *H.J.* Vol.42, p.45.

63 BETHARTOLI HIMAL, *east face (Harish Kapadia).*

63 BETHARTOLI HIMAL (6352 M)
Situated on the outer boundary of the Nanda Devi Sanctuary, the main peak was first attempted in 1950 by a Scottish team along its north ridge. A

German team recceed the northeast approaches in 1956; an Indian team attempted the south face in 1970 with three fatalities (including the famous Sherpa instructor, Ang Kami), while an American

team was defeated on the south face in 1977. Later in the same year an Italian team (R. Moro) made the first ascent via the north ridge. The south peak (6318 m) was first climbed by a German team (F. Hieber) in 1956 from the Bethartoli glacier, and has had two subsequent ascents.

64 SWARGAROHINI (6252 M)
The highest of a group of five, this peak forms the Path to Heaven, followed by the Pandavas, Draupadi and their dog. It has been attempted from both the Ruinsara valley as well as from the Jamdar Bamak in the Har-ki-doon valley. Swargarohini II (6247 m) was first climbed in 1974 by an Indo-Canadian team (Dr Charles Clarke). In 1985 an Indian party (Anil Kumar) made the second ascent and first of Swargarohini III (6209 m). In 1977 Indians climbed Swargarohini IV (5966 m).

64 SWARGAROHINI, *from the slopes of Kalanag (Harish Kapadia).*

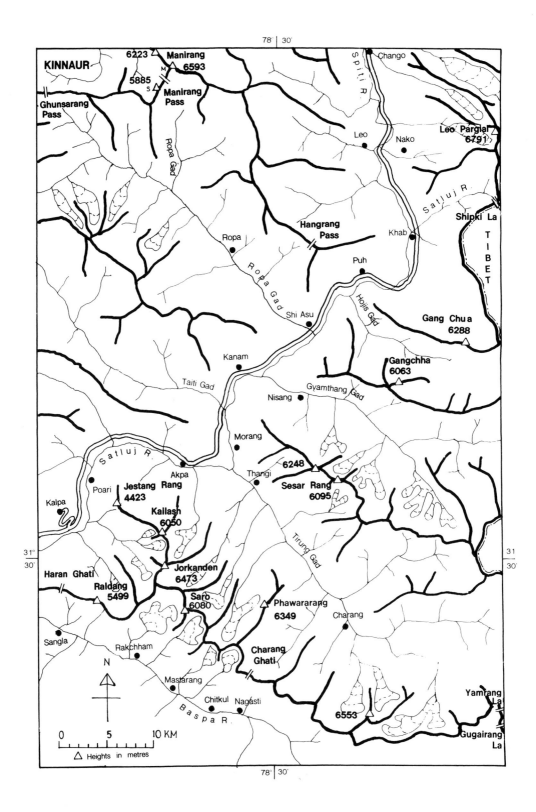

KINNAUR

6223 Manirang
              6593
5885   Manirang
M   Pass
S
Ghunsarang
Pass

Chango

Spiti R.

Leo   Nako   Leo Pargial
                              6791

Satluj R.

Ropa Gad

Hangrang
Pass   Khab   Shipki La

Ropa   T
                                                I
                    Puh   B
Ropa Gad   E
                                                 T

Shi Asu   Hojis Gad   Gang Chu a
                                    6288

Kanam   Gangchha
                                        6063

Taiti Gad   Gyamthang Gad

                Nisang

                Morang

Satluj R.   6248
            Akpa   Sesar Rang
Poari   Jestang Rang   Thangi   6095
            4423
Kalpa   Kailash
              6050
                                    Tirung Gad
Haran Ghati   Jorkanden
            Raldang   6473
              5499   Saro   Phawararang
                          6080   6349   Charang
Sangla   Rakchham
                                    Charang
                N   Ghati
            Mastarang
                    Chitkul Nagasti
                Baspa R.   Yamrang
                                                          La
0   5   10 KM   6553   Gugairang
                                                          La
△ Heights in metres

31°
30'

31
30'

78° 30'   78° 30'

3
KINNAUR

KINNAUR CONJURES UP A picture of inaccessible valleys, of the Hindustan-Tibet road, of the mighty gorge of Satluj and strange customs. It was where Rudyard Kipling's *Kim* travelled on his famous mission. But things have changed drastically since the time of *Kim*, and many possibilities for trekkers and mountaineers have opened up. While it previously took about two weeks of trekking to reach Kinnaur, the National Highway No. 22 now runs along the Satluj and is kept open almost throughout the year.

The earliest traveller-explorers to Kinnaur were the Gerard brothers in 1818.[1] Few others passed on the Hindustan-Tibet road. All the early writings are on how to reach Kinnaur and the dangers along the road.[2] It was left to Marco Pallis in 1933 to bring these valleys to the notice of mountaineers by an article[3] and a book[4] when he climbed Leo Pargial (6791 m), travelled on the Hindustan-Tibet road into the Baspa valley and crossed the Lamkhaga pass to Gangotri. There were many pilgrims who went around the (Kinnaur) Kailash massif, clockwise, from the Tirung valley, over Charang Ghati to Baspa and back and the tradition continues even today. The Army and the I.T.B.P., who were the only ones allowed into this restricted area until recently, have made many climbs.

Kalpa, situated in the centre of Kinnaur, is the district head-quarters, with one of the finest views one can have while enclosed in a comfortable bungalow. As Roy Chaud-hury writes, 'From the forest bungalow at Chini, 9400 feet above sea-level and 145 miles from Simla along the Hindustan-Tibet road, the Kailash massif is seen to advant-age. The snow-fields are so close that in spring the reflected light from the snows is painful to the eyes, while during the monsoon the sound of falling avalanches can be heard all day long.'[5]

Incidentally, the old name 'Chini' was changed to Kalpa, just in case the Chinese had some other ideas! About 760 m below Kalpa is Rekong Peo, which is developing as the central bazar and administrative town, served by many buses which pass on the Hindustan-Tibet road – from Shimla (old Simla) to Wangtu (where the Inner Line begins), Karchham (bifurcate southeast for Sangla, 17 km), Powari (for Rekong Peo, 6 km and Kalpa, 13 km), Akpa (for Morang and the Tirung valley), Kanam (for the Gyamthang valley), Shi Asu Khad (for the Ropa valley), Puh (old Poo), Leo and Chango (for Leo Pargial in the east). The motorable road continues to Kaurik and Sumdo to enter Spiti and reach Kaja.

An afternoon bus from Kalpa will reach Shimla on the same day and Chandigadh the next morning. These de-velopments have opened up many possibilities for the local people and the valleys are now far more accessible to mountaineers. Luckily it has not yet taken a heavy toll of the forest cover, culture and peace.

A lot has been written on the cultural aspect of Kinnaur. A fusion of Hinduism and Buddhism exists almost in totality. Every village has a temple and a gompa and all worship at both. Various primitive traditions, beliefs and superstitions survive. Legends are held in awe. Though a large proportion of the population is educated, and many serve in the Army, you may still be fined a sacrifice of a goat if you sit on a temple parapet with your shoes on! Human sacrifice was offered to the goddess in earlier times and one can see a special square built for the purpose. Now, animal sacrifice takes place regularly.[6]

Kinnauri architecture is a thing of beauty to behold. Perched on a hillock, the Kamru Fort or some exquisite gompas and temples can take one's breath away. The area also has plenty of fruit orchards and the valleys are rich and hospitable.

For such a large district, where people have travelled for years, it is not possible to record its mountain and mountaineering history exhaustively. What is attempted here is a brief resumé of possibilities in different valleys, an information update on approaches, based on recent travels, treks and climbs, and a few historical highlights.

The Satluj literally cuts through the Himalayan chain near Shipki la and then runs through the centre of Kinnaur. There are four major valleys to its southeast and east.

Baspa valley

Captain Conway called this 'the most lovely of all the Himalayan valleys'.[7] We would heartily agree with this. Many travellers have visited this valley, for it is connected to Garhwal in the south by some famous passes which have been crossed from time immemorial. The main ones are:

Buran Ghati: Sangla to Pabar gad
Rupin Ghati: Sangla to Rupin gad
Nargah Ghati: Sangla to Nargani khad
Singha Ghati: Mastarang to Supin gad
Khimloga Pass: Chhitkul to Supin gad
Borasu Ghati: Nagasti to Har-ki-Doon
Lamkhaga Pass: Upper Baspa valley to Harsil

All these passes offer possibilities for trekking, climbing small peaks and of grand views.

There are also two major passes which lead to Tibet. The famous one is the Yamrang la (5570 m) and a little to its south is the Gugairang la.

For mountaineers the upper Baspa valley offers a lot by way of shapely peaks. Generally they are all around 5600–5900 m with about five peaks rising above 6000 m and the highest up to 6227 m. Many have passed through this valley but the climbing history is brief, perhaps due to the lack of peaks of high enough altitude.

Col Balwant Sandhu led an expedition here in 1976 which climbed Pk 6215 m and another peak north of Sui Thatang.[8] Another visitor was Jack Gibson on two trekking

visits;[9] the Yamrang la was visited in 1978[10] and Soli
Mehta crossed the Lamkhaga pass with Maj Jungalwalla, in
1966.[11]

The I.T.B.P. have been in the area for many years, and
some officers have written warmly and authentically about
it.[12] But the two reported climbs in the Baspa valley which
include the three high peaks north of Dunthi have, unfortunately, no accurate written record.

A good motorable road branches off at Karchham to
Sangla. It is extended further to Rakchham, and Sushung
khad, four km short of Chhitkul. Buses ply regularly up to
Sangla and sometimes further up to Shushung khad. In a
year or two the road should reach Chhitkul.

Tirung valley (Tidong)

This valley north of Baspa has close connections with the
Baspa valley across the Charang Ghati (5242 m). It runs in
the east to the Khimokul la (Gunrang la) and Tibet. A
jeepable road leads from Morang to Thangi. Ahead, the
road is being constructed to Charang.

Thangi has been used as a starting point to attempt the
peaks in the Kinner-Kailash range. It also gives access to
Phawararang (6349 m) which has been climbed a few
times.[13] Northeast of Thangi lie two shapely peaks, both
awaiting climbers – Sesar Rang (6095 m) and the unnamed
Pk 6248 m, both on the Tirung-Gyamthang divide.

Kinner-Kailash range

There are three peaks to consider. First is Kailash (6050 m),
seen from Kalpa near the Shivling-shaped pillar which is
the real Kinner-Kailash, and worshipped as the holy summit. Finally there is Jorkanden (6473 m), the highest peak of
the massif, often mistaken for Kinner-Kailash.

Jorkanden has received various attempts and ascents.
After the recce by P. R. Oliver in 1931,[14] it was attempted by
the Indian Army in 1964, 1967, 1972, and in 1973 by Major
D. K. Khullar.[15] The first ascent was made in 1974 by the
I.T.B.P.[16] followed a month later by the Army.[17] Since
then, it has been climbed by the Indian Army again in 1978
led by the late Major Kiran Kumar.[18]

Gyamthang valley (Nisang)
A relatively unknown valley to the north of Tirung Gad is
approached from Kanam. It leads to the Raniso pass (into
Tibet) and has one peak of note, the 6063 m high Gangchha. Further to the east lies Gang Chua (6288 m). It was
climbed in 1974 by an Army team from the Hojis Lungba
valley to the north.[19] To the north of this there are no
mountains of great height till the Shipki la and the gorge
of the Satluj and its meeting with the Spiti river north of
Puh.

Leo Pargial (Hangrang valley)
This peak at 6791 m is a high landmark north of the Shipki
la on the Tibetan border, and has attracted mountaineers
for many years. It was reported to be recceed by the Gerard
brothers in 1818 and was first climbed by Marco Pallis and
C. B. M. Warren in 1933. It was attempted several times by
the Army, and climbed by them in 1967, 1975 and 1980.[20]
The I.T.B.P. made the third ascent in 1971.
    The peak has been frequently attempted by civilian
parties and was climbed twice in 1982.[21] Its principal
approach is from Nako and another route has been recceed
from Chango.[22] There are numerous six-thousanders
around it for the keen climbers. Discussions about its
correct name and height[23] were all laid to rest by the latest
Survey of India map (1975) which has adopted the above
spelling and height.

Northwest Kinnaur
To the northwest of the Satluj lies the other half of Kinnaur.
The gentler valleys lead to a divide with Pin valley (Spiti). It
has numerous passes which afford many a pleasurable
trekking route but offer no climbing higher than about 5900
m. The important passes are:
    Tari Khango pass: Bhabha valley to Pin-Parbati pass.
        (outside map)
    Larsa Way pass: Larsa Garang (Taiti Garang) to Pin
        valley.
    Ghunsarang pass: Ropa valley to Pin valley.
    Manirang pass: Ropa valley (to the north) to Pin valley.

It was over the Tari Khango that the Indo-New Zealand Himalayan Traverse Expedition passed in 1981,[24] a good pass for trekkers.

Historically, Dr J. de V. Graaff reached Manirang pass in 1952 and climbed Manirang peak (6593 m) to its northeast. Its second ascent was in 1988 by the Indian Para Regiment (Col B. S. Sandhu). The only other peaks climbed in the area are Manirang South in 1982[25] and 1986[26] and the unnamed Pk 6223 m to the north of Manirang, in 1973.[27] There are numerous peaks around 5500 m to 6000 m in the area which have not been touched. It is evident that in Kinnaur many trekking and climbing opportunities await the mountaineer. There are many side valleys, peaks and passes which are inviting, unexplored and certainly unre-corded. With the development of roads, the valleys of this beautiful district are one night away from Shimla.[28] Of course one has to solve the problem of the Inner Line permits, lack of porters and lack of information. But then it is no paradise which is gained easily. Even Kim had to hustle with Hurree babu to gain access here.

KINNAUR REFERENCES
1 *H.J.* Vol.II, p.73.
2 *H.J.* Vol.I, p.67.
3 *H.J.* Vol.VI, p.106.
4 *Peaks and Lamas*, Marco Pallis, London, 1939.
5 *Temples and Legends of Himachal Pradesh*, P. C. Roy Chaudhury, Bombay, 1981.
6 *H.J.* Vol.II, p.81.
7 *Sunlit Waters*, Capt C. W. W. S. Conway, Bombay, 1942.
8 *H.J.* Vol.XXXV, p.224.
9 *As I Saw It*, Jack Gibson, New Delhi, 1976.
10 *H.J.* Vol.36, p.193.
11 *H.J.* Vol.XXVIII, p.55.
12 'Land The Ogress Stalked: Kinnaur', D. S. Malik, *I.T.B.P. Bulletin*, July–Sept., 1975.
13 *H.J.* Vol.36, p.99; Vol.42, p.177.
14 *H.J.* Vol.IV, p.147.
15 *H.J.* Vol.XXXII, p.105.
16 Led by D. S. Malik; on 26 May, 1974.
17 Led by S. S. Kalhan; on 19 June, 1974.
18 *Kinner-Kailash Expedition*, Maj K. I. Kumar, New Delhi, 1979.
19 *H.J.* Vol.XXXIV, p.75.
20 1967: Col D. K. Khullar (second ascent); 1975: Brig J. Singh; 1980: Maj K. I. Kumar.
21 1982: P. Dasgupta (Bengal) and U. Sathe (Maharashtra).

22 *H.J.* Vol.38, p.95; Vol.39, p.195.
23 *H.J.* Vol.VI, p.106; Vol.XXVII, pp.182, 184; Vol.38, p.102.
24 *First Across the Roof of the World*, Graeme Dingle and Peter Hillary, Auckland, 1984.
25 *H.C.N.L.* 36, p.24.
26 *H.J.* Vol.43, p.66.
27 *H.C.N.L.* 30, p.13.
28 *Kinnaur* (Himachal Pradesh District Gazetteers), edited by M. D. Mamgain, 1971.

65 PARILUNGBI, *south ridge (Harish Kapadia).*

65 PARILUNGBI (6166 M)
A Mountain in the Other Country – such peaks were used as landmarks on the border; here between Spiti and Ladakh. They were also trade posts. On the summit of this peak stands a survey pole (Parang la Station 1). It is situated at the head of the Lingti valley-Yangzi Diwan pass, overlooking the Parang la trade route. It was climbed in 1987 by an Indian team (Harish Kapadia).

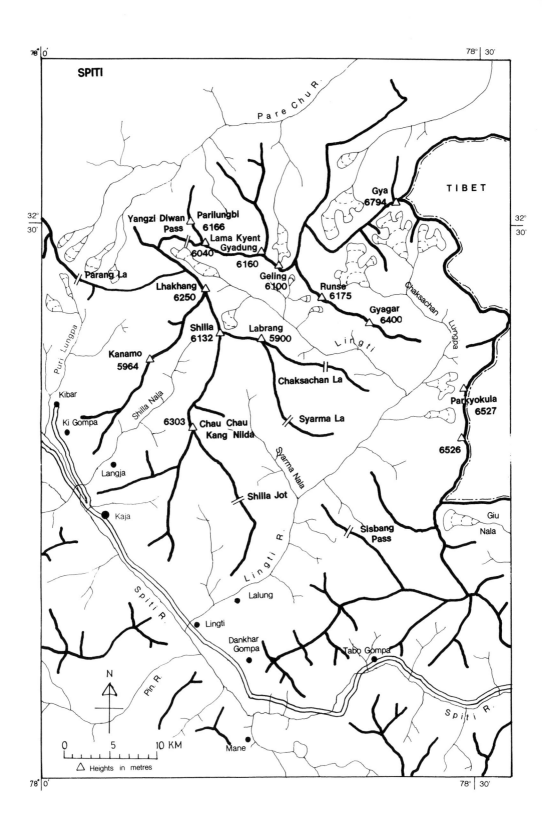

SPITI

Pare Chu R.

TIBET

Gya
6794

Yangzi Diwan
Pass
Parilungbi
6166
Lama Kyent
Gyadung
6040
6160
Geling
6100
Parang La
Lhakhang
6250
Runse
6175
Chaksachan Lungpa
Gyagar
6400
Shilla
6132
Labrang
5900
L i n g t i
Kanamo
5964
Chaksachan La
Parkyokula
6527
Kibar
Ki Gompa
6303
Chau Chau
Kang Nilda
Syarma La
6526
Langja
Syarma Nala
Kaja
Shilla Jot
Giu
Nala
Sisbang
Pass
Lingti R.
Lalung
Lingti
Dankhar
Gompa
Tabo Gompa
Spiti R.
N
Pin R.
Spiti R.
0   5   10 KM
Mane
△ Heights in metres

Puri Lungpa

Shilla Nala

4
SPITI

S PITI LITERALLY means 'middle country' and it
is so named as it lies across the main Himalayan
chain, between Tibet and India. It can also be
considered the land between the Satluj gorge and
the river systems of the Chenab and Beas (three of the five
rivers that comprise Punjab, lower in the plains).

The Spiti river flows in a rough northwest/southeast
direction, cutting the valley into its eastern and western
halves. It flows into the mighty Satluj, which carves out a
most formidable gorge for itself as it enters India near the
Shipka la, about ten km from Puh (old Poo). The confluence of the two is at Khab.

As we proceed upstream from the confluence, on its
eastern bank, we first meet the remarkable river system of
the Pare Chu which rises to the north of the Parang la, and
travels some thirty km eastwards, then turns sharp south to
enter Tibet for a further eighty-five km and then, as
suddenly, switches to a westerly course to re-enter India at
Kaurik and merge into the Spiti near Sumdo (off the map) –
a unique path for a fast flowing river at such heights. A little
higher up, also not far from Sumdo, and on the eastern bank
we meet the Giu nala. Next is the valley of the Lingti, the
largest tributary of the Spiti, which it meets at the village of
Lingti. This valley is sixty km long, and at its northern end,
on the Tibetan border, stands Gya (6794 m), the highest
peak in Himachal Pradesh – for the record it is three metres

higher than Leo Pargial. Further up towards the source lies
Kaja (old Kaza) the administrative headquarters of Spiti.
Above Kaja lie the Shilla nala and the Puri lungpa which
leads to the Parang la (5600 m) and finally the Takling nala
which flows down from the Takling la. The source of the
Spiti lies at the foot of the Kunzam la. Both the Parang and
Takling las separate Spiti from the Rupshu district of
Ladakh, while the path over the Kunzum la leads into
Lahul.

The western section of Spiti adjoins Kulu and Kinnaur.
Proceeding upstream from the confluence with the Satluj,
the first large tributary is the Pin which joins the Spiti a little
distance from the Lingti confluence (on the opposite bank).
Several passes – the Manirang, Ghunsarang, Tari Khango
and Shakraode – lead into Kinnaur, while the famous Pin-
Parbati pass allows access into the beautiful valley of Parbati
in Kulu.

The Pin river has the Parahio nala as its main tributary,
and then further upstream the Spiti is joined by the Ratang
and Gyundi nalas which are completely cut off from the
Kulu side. It is proposed to declare the Gyundi valley a
National Park. Access will then be forbidden in order to
prevent the denudation of flora and fauna.

Spiti first came to the notice of the outside world in 1945
when H. M. Paidar and L. Schmaderer escaped British
wartime internment and followed in the footsteps of
Heinrich Harrer and Peter Aufschnaiter. Alas, they decided
to turn back and it was on their return, at Tabo in Spiti, that
Schmaderer was robbed and murdered. Not knowing that
the war was over, Paidar followed the Satluj to Saharan
where he gave himself up and reported the incident to the
police. The murderers were subsequently arrested. It was
Spiti's first criminal blot in forty years.[1]

Let us briefly review the expeditions that have visited
Spiti. We'll start with the now famous *khalasi* of the Survey
of India who held a survey pole atop Shilla in 1860. He
became the unnamed hero, even if his height record proved
to be an error, created by those who were measuring the
angles from below. Much later came J. O. M. Roberts in
1939 when, after his wanderings in Kulu, he crossed over

the Pin Parbati Pass and explored the Shilla nala. In the process of examining the approaches to Shilla, he climbed Guan Nelda (now renamed Chau Chau Kang Nilda, or C.C.K.N. for short).[2]

In 1952 J. de V. Graaff and K. Snelson also recceed the area around Shilla, but serious exploration really starts with the expeditions of P. F. Holmes in 1955 and 1956. On the first trip, he and T. H. Braham entered Spiti over the Kunzum la and climbed Pk $c.5485$ m near the Kunzum la, and Pk $c.5945$ m along with Pk $c.6100$ m, both near the pass between the Ratang and Parahio valleys. They also climbed C.C.K.N. Shilla was reduced to its proper size and yet another Himalayan mystery was solved. The following year, Holmes climbed several peaks which included Ratang Tower (6340 m) and other smaller five to six-thousanders in the Ratang and Gyundi valleys. It was an exceptional piece of exploration of an area where previous surveys appeared to have been expressed on the maps purely by imagination.[3]

Nothing happened for another ten years until in 1966 an Indian team (R. Jaikumar) climbed Shilla (by now accurately marked as 6132 m), C.C.K.N. (6380 m), Kanikma (now Kanamo) (5965 m) and a rock tower ($c.6100$ m) near Shilla.[4] Again there was a five-year gap until 1981 when two Indian students, M. H. Contractor and R. Vohra, climbed C.C.K.N.[5] Muslim Contractor must obviously have spread the word about the exciting prospects in the still little known area because he became a member of the Bombay team (H. B. Kapadia) which spent a good five weeks in Spiti in 1983, during which time they climbed Langma (5761 m), Sibu ($c.5700$ m), Zumto ($c.5800$ m), Tserip ($c.5890$ m) and Kawu ($c.5910$ m). They also attempted Tangmor ($c.5900$ m) and Shijbang ($c.5250$ m) – the names of the last six peaks are expedition names and their heights are altimeter readings. Finally an attempt on C.C.K.N. was beaten back.[6]

The next few years saw Indian expeditions to Shilla, climbed (S. Bhattacharya)[7] and attempted (S. Roy Chaudhury) in 1985; and to C.C.K.N., climbed in 1985 and 1986 by teams led by B. P. Roy and N. Chakraborty, respectively.

More recently (in 1987) Harish Kapadia completed a task left unfinished in 1983. The 1987 expedition to Spiti comprehensively explored the Lingti valley and identified and located Gya (6794 m). They crossed the Yangzi Diwan pass (5890 m) and climbed Parilungbi (6166 m) lying across the watershed in Ladakh, attempted Shilla initially from the north and also from its eastern col, and made the first ascents of Lama Kyent (6040 m), Labrang (*c*.5900 m), Runse (6175 m), Geling (*c*.6100 m) and Gyadung (6160 m). They also attempted Lhakhang (6250 m) and Gyagar (*c*.6400 m). Altogether a pioneering piece of work in the old tradition.[8]

The accessibility of Spiti has improved a hundredfold, as has the knowledge of its geography. Spiti, anyone?

SPITI REFERENCES
1 *H.J.* Vol.XV, p.69.
2 *H.J.* Vol.XII, p.129.
3 *H.J.* Vol.XX, p.78; *Mountains and a Monastery*, P. F. Holmes, London, 1958.
4 *H.J.* Vol.XXVII, p.185; *H.C.N.L.* 24, p.5.
5 *H.J.* Vol.39, p.198; *H.C.N.L.* 35, p.25.
6 *H.J.* Vol.40, p.96.
7 *H.J.* Vol.42, p.190.
8 *H.J.* Vol.44, p.96.

66 KISHTWAR SHIVLING (*c*.6000 M)
The peak became more well known after the fine elegant first ascent of its north face by Stephen Venables and Dick Renshaw in 1983. The peak still retains many more variations, each of which would give as much satisfaction to the skilled climber as the original route of ascent.

67 AGYASOL (6200 M)
A beautiful peak climbed by a British team (Simon Richardson) in 1981 by the north face. The only other attempt (in 1980) by a British team failed.

66 KISHTWAR SHIVLING *from Upper Umasi glacier (Stephen Venables).*

67 AGYASOL, *north face (Stephen Venables).*

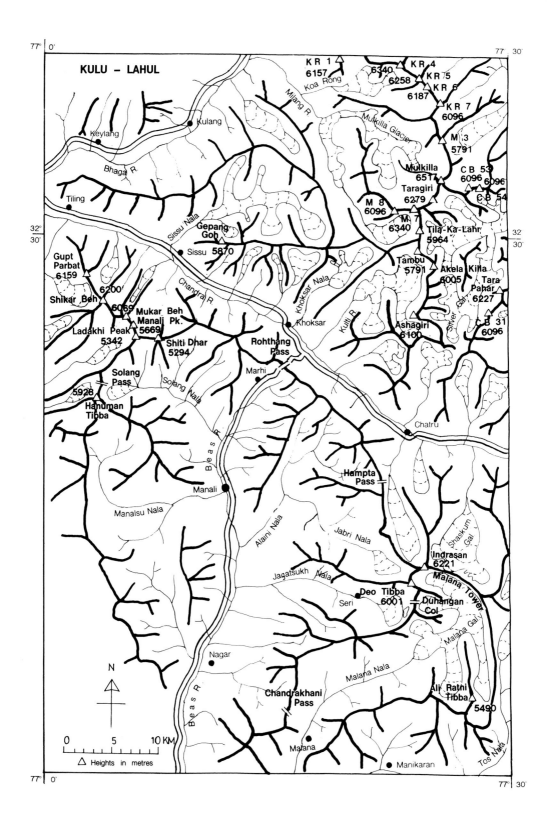

KULU – LAHUL

KR 1
6157

6340

KR 4

KR 5
6258

KR 6
6187

KR 7
6096

Koa Rong

Milang R.

Mulkilla Glacier

M 3
5791

Mulkilla
6517

CB 53
6096 6096

Taragiri
6279

CB 54

M 8
6096

M 7
6340

Tila-Ka-Lahr
5964

Keylang

Kulang

Bhaga R.

Tiling

Sissu Nala

Gepang
Goh

Tambu
5791

Akela Killa
6005

Tara
Pahar
6227

Gupt
Parbat
6159

Sissu 5870

Chandra R.

Khoksar Nala

Kulti R.

Ashagiri
6100

Silver Col

CB 31
6096

Shikar Beh

6200

6069

Mukar Beh
Manali Pk.
5669

Khoksar

Ladakhi Peak
5342

Shiti Dhar
5294

Rohthang
Pass

Solang
Pass

Marhi

5928

Solang Nala

Hanuman
Tibba

Beas R.

Chatru

Hampta
Pass

Manali

Manalsu Nala

Alaini Nala

Jabri Nala

Shaskum Gal

Indrasan
6221

Jagatsukh Nala

Malana Tower

Deo Tibba
6001

Seri

Duhangan
Col

Malana Gal

N

Nagar

Beas R.

Malana Nala

Ali Ratni
Tibba
5490

Chandrakhani
Pass

0   5   10 KM

△ Heights in metres

Malana

Manikaran

Tos Nala

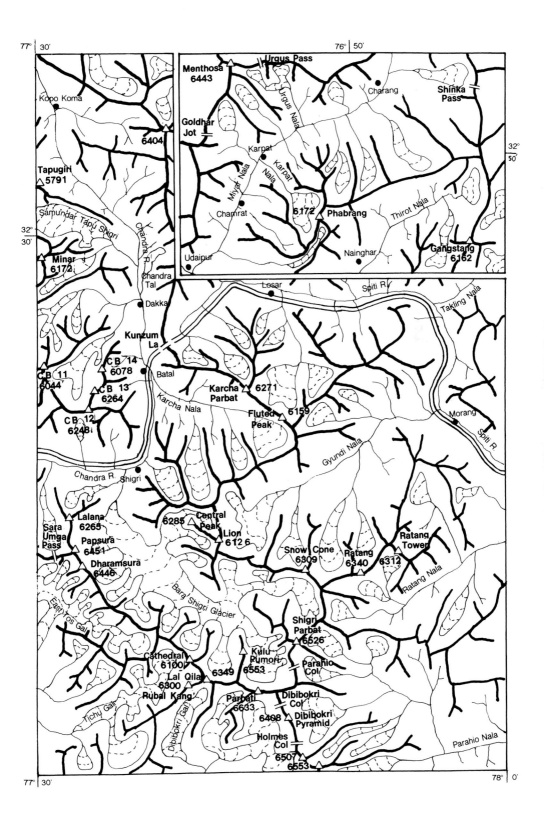

5

KULU AND
LAHUL

T
HE KULU VALLEY has been a happy hunting
ground (literally) for shikaris, trekkers and
climbers alike. Before the construction of the
motor road, the most popular routes were over the
passes on the Dhauladhar range from Mandi State. One
could also travel in ten easy stages from Shimla, via
Narkanda, Larji and Bajaura.[1]

The valley is dominated by the river Beas which rises at
the Rohthang pass, and by its major tributary Parbati which
originates in the glacier system around the Pin-Parbati pass
separating Kulu from Spiti. The L formation of the two
rivers contains a mountain area on both sides of the arms
which could keep the active mountaineer busy for over a
score of seasons.

Over the Rohthang pass lies Lahul, a district almost
totally bounded by the rivers Chandra and Bhaga which
eventually merge in the southwest corner to become the
Chenab.

Today, motorable roads can carry the visitor from
Pathankot to Manali, Shimla to Manali, Manali to Kaja
(in Spiti and thence via the Satluj gorge back to Shimla),
Manali to the Baralacha pass (and beyond to Leh in Ladakh)
or down the Chenab to Kishtwar. Ease of access to the
mountains of one's choice is an important reason for the
popularity of Kulu. The only loss that the increase in traffic
has brought to the valley is the total disappearance of its
wildlife which at some distant point in the past could boast
of being a paradise for the shikari. Alas, if you happen to

come across some pug marks today, they are more likely to be that of the Yeti than those of the brown bear!

East of the river Beas and up to its barrier wall with Spiti lies the major climbing arena of glaciers, interconnected between themselves by passes so that a variety of approaches can be attempted. Thus the Indrasan-Deo Tibba area can be equally well approached from the Jagatsukh nala (off the Beas) as from the Malana nala. The Parbati valley has three tributaries, the head of each being a climber's playground – Tichu, Tos and Dibibokri. The mountains at their head go up to the high ridge that separates them from the Bara Shigri glacier which is approached from across the Rohthang or Hampta passes and into Lahul and the eastern end of the Chandra loop. East of Bara Shigri lies the Gyundi nala complex in Spiti.

A word about the Dhaula Dhar would not be out of place in this chapter. Dhaula Dhar is a mountain wall separating the Kangra and the Kulu valleys. Indeed, the passes over this moderate range were the preferred bridle routes in the days before motorable roads. From the comforts of Dharamsala one can reach the upper grazing grounds and the mountains in two to three marches. The area was a weekend climber's paradise and many of the modest summits have been climbed. J. O. M. Roberts with C. D. Buckle took ten days off in 1937 and their description is likely to whet a number of appetites.[2]

Some of the earliest climbing in Kulu was done by C. G. Bruce who, with the Swiss guide Heinrich Fuhrer and some Gurkhas from his regiment, spent six happy months climbing and exploring in the area in 1912. His books[3] make fascinating reading and should be mandatory for all those who visit Kulu, despite the fact that heights and names of peaks have changed since they were published.

They climbed in the Solang nala and made the first ascent of Hanuman Tibba (christened the Solang Weisshorn for its similarity to the peak in the Alps). They made several recces around Deo Tibba but were singularly unfortunate with the weather and snow conditions. As the monsoon hit the valley, they crossed over into Lahul and climbed Gepang Goh (which Bruce likened to the Schreckhorn in the Alps), then moved up the Bhaga, past Keylang and Darcha to a base near Patseo and climbed several peaks in the area. Another excursion was up the Parbati valley and his description can with some difficulty be matched with the place names and peaks we recognise today on our modern maps. Part of his Lahul adventure was shared with Capt Todd who joined them for some time.

Deo Tibba was the prime attraction in the early years of serious climbing in Kulu, possibly because of its proximity to Manali and also the prominent way it displayed itself from nearby view points.

But it was twenty-seven years before J. O. M. Roberts took over in 1939,[4] where Bruce had left off. Ascending the beautiful Jagatsukh valley, he reached the pass (now Duhangan col) that opens to the southeast of Deo Tibba and leads onto the névés of the Malana glacier. Access to the summit was barred by a transverse ridge and further exploration was given up, but Roberts' conclusion was that the Malana glacier could possibly provide a route to the top.

In 1940 Capt L. C. Lind pottered round the area and left some useful notes with Maj Banon (Hon. local secretary of the Himalayan Club) in Manali – alas Lind was killed shortly after, in the battle for Singapore. Not much is known of the attempt of three Italian prisoners of war (Bianchini, Mamini and Fuselli) who, on their release in 1945, ascended the Malana glacier to attempt Deo Tibba; having failed to do so, they climbed Pk 5510 m (18,076 ft on the old map) and having left a replica of the lion of St Mark on the summit, named the peak 'Punta San Marco'.

1950 and the following years saw some quite feverish activity to solve the Deo Tibba problem (apparently so easy, but protected by lousy snow conditions and bad weather). E. H. Peck and C. R. Patterson,[5] followed the Bruce route via the Jabri nala and Pianguru thach and pushed further up the glacier and onto its lower plateau. Here they were confronted with the precipices of the southern bastions of the mountain. Peck returned the next year with his wife and repeated Roberts' traverse up to the Duhangan col but, having run short of time, they consoled themselves with an ascent of Pk 5229 m (17,155 ft on the old map) which rises to the south of the pass. That same year (1951), R. C. Evans, A. G. Trower and E. Ker again approached the Duhangan route and investigated the two ridges to the southeast and south of the peak. The former they named the 'Piton ridge' (a piton had been found on it) and the southern ridge was christened the 'Watershed ridge' being on the watershed of Malana and Duhangan valleys. After a false start on the Piton ridge, they set up camp on the Watershed ridge and were well on their way to the summit but just before arriving at the vast glacier dome (west of Punta San Marco), the snow suddenly became soft, deep and treacherous and that was the end of that gallant attempt. As consolation the trio made the first ascent of Pk 4973 m (16,316 ft on the old map) and two neighbouring summits to the east, on their return to Seri.

Deo Tibba couldn't possibly hold out much longer and in 1952 a team led by J. de V. Graaff, with his wife and K. E. Berrill, were luckier than their predecessors. With their base at Seri, they quickly gained the Piton ridge and followed it over (or past) the Punta San Marco to a stiff snow ramp which eventually led them to the ridge connecting to the upper névés. C3 was set on these névés (c.5545 m). The next day an hour's trudge brought them near the glacier saddle between Deo Tibba and Indrasan. From this point a wide snow crest, splattered here and there with crevasses and ice-walls, rose to the summit which they reached (unfortunately in fog), six hours after leaving camp.

Graaff also had his eye on Indrasan but the monsoon had arrived and prevented further adventures. But earlier in the season Graaff, his wife and Snelson had climbed two summits in the Dibibokri nala (off Parbati), one of which was a first ascent named Rubal Kang, Turtle Peak (c.6300 m), and the other of 5850 m; they crossed several passes into Spiti and explored the approaches to Shilla which they failed to climb, but ascended Manirang (6598 m) on the frontier of Bushair.

Indrasan (6221 m), Deo Tibba's immediate neighbour initially excited less interest and was merely marked as Pk 20,410 ft on the old map. It took the more adventurous of those eyeing Deo Tibba to have a go at this rock castle also.

It was not until 1958 that H. McArthur and Maj G. Douglas made a serious attempt, followed by Robert Pettigrew with the Derbyshire expedition of 1961.[6] It was the Kyoto University Alpine Club (Prof K. Onodera) who finally made the first ascent in 1962 having also climbed Deo Tibba on the same day.[7] From C3 on the upper névé of the Malana glacier, they found a route up the intricacies of the south face rather than trudge the long and exposed west ridge. The second summit team managed to reach the top in deteriorating weather and bivouacked on their way down before reaching the safety of C3, which was also the jumping off point for the ascent of Deo Tibba.

A smaller climbing playground, but no less interesting, is that of the Solang nala, north of Manali. It is dominated by Hanuman Tibba (5928 m), Bruce's Solang Weisshorn, but the cirque also has the more modest Ladakhi Peak (5342 m) from which a ridge runs north to Manali Peak (5669 m) and onto Mukar Beh (6069 m) and Shikar Beh (6200 m); then back in the main arena is Shiti Dhar (5294 m) and Goh Kincha (5153 m), and still lesser heights for the novice to cut his teeth on. After Bruce's ascent, the second ascent of Hanuman Tibba was made by a team of friends led by R. Pettigrew in 1966[8] by its south ridge. Several climbs have since been made of this favourite mountain. Mukar Beh, however, is a much more tough proposition; not only does one traverse over Manali Peak but from then onwards, the connecting ridge is of the worst type – well corniced, loose rock and soft snow – which gave the climbers on the first ascent a harrowing time. These were John Ashburner and the indomitable Ladakhi Wangyal in 1968.[9]

The Parbati valley is beautiful in its own right as a trekker's dream, but the keen climber has the Tos, Tichu and the Dibibokri nalas to keep him occupied with excellent prospects and variations of routes. This area along with the peaks of the Malana glacier to the west is difficult to cover comprehensively – so numerous are the possibilities. At the head of the Malana nala lie 'Malana Towers' one of which was first climbed by Colin Pritchard's party in 1966,[10] after they had sent two successful ropes up Deo Tibba lying immediately to the east. The other landmark of interest in

the Malana glacier is of course the granite obelisk of Ali
Ratni Tibba (5490 m), which was treated with great respect
by the early visitors to the area. With the techniques of
climbing improving as the years passed by, it was bound to
fall to strong climbers, which it did in 1969 when Fred
Harper, Mrs M. A. Harper, D. Nicoll and C. Radcliffe got
to the top by its west ridge.[11] The same year Deo Tibba
suffered (in silence one presumes) a mass ascent of twenty-
four climbers led by Giuseppe Tenti. Malana nala also
possesses its 'Manikaran Spires' which should keep the new
breed of technicians busy.

Of the three tributaries of the Parbati, the Dibibokri was
the first to be investigated,[12] by K. Snelson in 1952, along
with Graaff and Schelpe. The map of those days was
hopelessly inaccurate and they not only climbed, but explored around this valley thoroughly. They climbed and
named 'Rubal Kang' (Turtle Peak) and 'Ratiruni Pyramid'
at the head of the subsidiary Ratiruni glacier, explored right
up to the Parahio watershed and returned to the main
Parbati by a short-cut southeast of the Ratiruni Pyramid. Pk
6633 m (21,760 ft) dominates the whole of the Kulu-Lahul
area. Several teams had their eye on this highest summit in
the region and its first ascent was made by an Italian team
led by M. Tremonti in 1968[13] who appropriately named it
'Parbati Parbat'. They approached the peak from the main
Dibibokri glacier, onto a col separating the peak and the
Dibibokri Pyramid to its southeast and then followed the
connecting ridge to the top, a remarkable achievement on a
peak that had only a few years ago been described as
extremely tough (which it still is). The Dibibokri nala had
also been a happy hunting ground for an earlier Italian team
in 1961[14] led by P. Consiglio who, amongst further exploration, climbed Pk 6349 m (20,830 ft) – a magnificent tower of
rock with almost vertical walls which they named 'Lal Qila'
(Red Fort) from its reddish granite. It is marked in some
maps as Kulu Makalu.

The Tos nala has an equally challenging array of peaks,
the prominent and much attempted being Papsura (6451 m)
which is a few metres higher than its neighbour Dharamsura (6446 m), or White Sail as it was earlier known. The

legend has it that the two mountains gain ascendency over each other according to whether the forces of evil (*Pap*) or those of good (*Dharm*) happen to prevail over the world at the time. So now we know! Dharamsura had been climbed by J. O. M. Roberts way back in 1940. Its second ascent was twenty-one years later by the Derbyshire expedition of 1961 (R. Pettigrew). Papsura eventually received its first ascent by R. Pettigrew's party in 1967[15] when Geoff Hill and Colin Pritchard made a bold sortie up the western couloir of its south face, at a time when most of the team were *hors de combat*, Pettigrew in particular from a hip dislocated when an earlier attempt ended with an avalanche dragging the climbers to the lip of the bergschrund.

Let us cross over the Rohthang Pass into Lahul. Straight ahead, prominently visible from the pass itself is the Kulti nala where the first serious climbing and exploration was provided by the R.A.F. Mountaineering Association Expedition (A. J. M. Smyth) in 1955.[16] They opened the area to thorough knowledge and climbed several peaks which they appropriately named. It has since then been popular with expeditions who have little time to spare. Above the Chandra river, between Sissu and Gondla lies Gepang Goh (5870 m), first climbed by Gen Bruce with the Swiss guide Heinrich Fuhrer and two Gurkhas in July 1912. The second ascent was 42 years later, in September 1954, by N. Wollaston and R. Platts. The peak is not as easy as it looks.

Round the corner, on the Bhaga arm of the region off Darcha lies another valley, the Milang nala with its smaller tributaries, the Tela and Koa Rong. The opening of this climbing arena was the work of the National Union of Students' team led by L. Krenek, in 1939. Inspired by Bruce's book and S.O.I. sheet 52H, which only had one peak of 21,380 ft (Mulkila) marked on it, they decided to approach it via the Milang. They numbered the peaks nala-wise – M1 etc for the peaks in the Milang nala, the prefix KR for those in the Koa Rong and T for the Tela valley. They climbed their main target Mulkila (M4) and also M7 and M3. Their report[17] has been standard reference for all subsequent expeditions, of which there have been several.

Again of recent knowledge, the CB (Chandra Bhaga)

group lies at the heart of Central Lahul and extends up to its southeastern corner. The westernmost peaks of the CB group adjoin and share common ridges with the Kulti and the Milang nala summits.[18] A number of these summits can also be approached from further up the Chandra, near Chandra Tal, where the Samundar Tapu Shigri (glacier) ends. Only a few of the CB peaks have been climbed – CB12, CB31, CB46, CB47, CB53 and CB54. So here again a vast collection of unclimbed peaks between 5000– 6000 m await the enterprising climber.

We leave the valleys for a while and describe the climbing arena of the Bara Shigri glacier. Visited by A. E. Gunther in 1953,[19] the initial impression created by the likes of J. O. M. Roberts, P. F. Holmes and T. H. Braham who climbed along the periphery of Bara Shigri from its adjacent valleys, prompted a ladies' team led by Joyce Dunsheath to make one of the first serious traverses of the Bara Shigri glacier in 1956, exploring, surveying and climbing some of the peaks that abound in this vast amphitheatre of glaciation.[20] (All this was while P. F. Holmes and T. H. Braham were filling the blanks on the map across the watershed in the Gyundi and Ratang valleys in Spiti.) J. P. O'F. Lynam came next in 1961[21] and cleared up some more anomalous heights and positions in the Bara Shigri and its divide with the Gyundi. It takes the researcher some time to unravel the different surveys of the expedition and not until a reliable Survey of India sheet of recent origin is referred to can one mark the peaks climbed and reconcile their heights and positions (not to mention names) for future climbers. Several expeditions have visited this area, each picking on an unclimbed sum- mit. For example in 1964 R. Pettigrew[22] and Dr F. Mohling came up and camped at what is now popularly known as Concordia. Then, with an astute bit of route-finding, they picked on the southwest ridge of Kulu Pumori (6553 m) and made a first ascent in fine style, all four of the expedition (the other two being Ladakhis Wangyal and Angchuk) reaching the summit on 6 and 9 June, 1964. Gradually the Bara Shigri peaks are receiving their baptism by small parties of keen climbers but the supply of unclimbed peaks, ridges and faces is large enough to last out for some decades!

A word can be said here about the average Ladakhi porter available to expeditions in the Kulu-Lahul area. They are hardy and some are fully up to the standards expected of the Sherpas of the eastern Himalaya. In the early days – the 1950s and 1960s – a few Ladakhis proved to be outstanding climbers. Wangyal was described by Bob Pettigrew as a superb mountaineer and an unfailing guide, and Rikzen (Ringzing) who, with Holmes and Braham was atop every summit in 1955, was judged by Holmes as 'in a class by himself'. These opinions were echoed by all teams fortunate enough to engage their services and they will be long remembered as playing a prominent role in the expeditions and explorations that were carried out in their active days.

As we leave Lahul and follow the Chenab (Chandra-Bhaga) westwards from the confluence at Tandi, we come to the small township of Udaipur close to which the Miyar nala flows into the Chenab. This valley has a number of climbing prospects, although the main targets to date have been Menthosa (6444 m), Baihali Jot (6280 m), Duphao Jot (6100 m) and Phabrang (6172 m). Serious climbing started here with the Indo-British expedition (Maj H. V. Bahuguna) of 1969.[23] A brave attempt on Menthosa fell short of the summit by a hundred feet, but they made the first ascents of Baihali and Duphao Jots and an unnamed summit Pk 5784 m (18,977 ft). Since then the area has been well visited,[24] and exploration has continued up the other tributaries of the Miyar valley. The Gumba and the Palphu nalas used to be unknown even to the cognoscenti of the Himalayan Club! In 1980, the ladies of the Pinnacle Club showed us how it is to be done – a thoroughly detailed exploration led by Sheila Cormack opened our eyes to the possibilities in the Gumba,[25] and in 1983, Geoff Cohen did likewise in the Palphu,[26] both teams climbing extensively in their area of choice. Several such side nalas await the enterprising climber and trekker.

Finally a 'new' area has also been brought to light, that lying to the south of the Parbati river and up to the Pin-Parbati Pass. It can be approached either from the Parbati side and its tributary glaciers or from the Sainj nala, and over a col north of Pk c.5640 m (c.18,500 ft) (Snowy Peak).

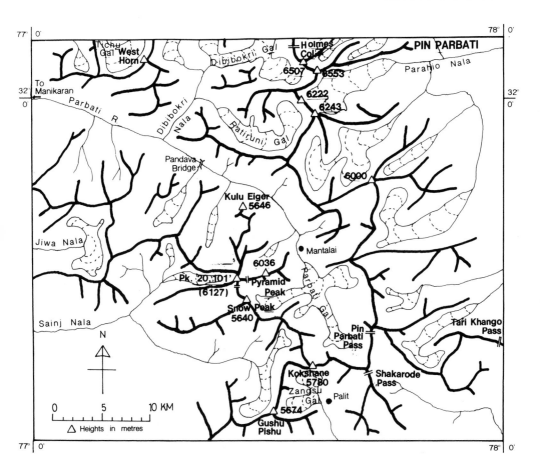

Charles Ainger and Iain Ogilvie 'discovered' this region in 1970, again aided by a very inaccurate S.O.I. sheet.[27] They climbed a few peaks in the area, but in 1973 their useful survey prompted Rob Collister, hemmed in by restrictions up the Parbati, to force his way up the Sainj valley over the col mentioned above, to make a fine ascent of Pk 6127 m (Pk 20,101 ft on most old maps), the highest peak in the area. Collister's team then gorged themselves with several ascents – the others in the happy party being Isherwood, Cardy and Cohen.[28]

The amphitheatre that comprises the valleys and glaciers bounded by the Chandra (in the north), Beas (in the east) and Parbati (in the south) up to the watershed with Spiti (in the west), still harbours endless possibilities.

KULU AND LAHUL REFERENCES

1 *H.J.* Vol.V, pp.75, 85.
2 *H.J.* Vol.X, p.164.
3 *Kulu and Lahoul*, C. G. Bruce, London, 1914; *Himalayan Wanderer*, C. G. Bruce, London, 1934.
4 *Mountain World* 1954 (Ed. M. Kurz), p.217.
5 *H.J.* Vol.XVII, p.118; see also p.126.
6 *H.J.* Vol.XXIII, p.110.
7 *H.J.* Vol.XXIV, p.90.
8 *H.J.* Vol.XXVII, p.94.
9 *H.J.* Vol.XXVIII, p.21.
10 *Ibid.* p.8.
11 *H.J.* Vol.XXX, p.212.
12 *H.J.* Vol.XVIII, p.110.
13 *H.J.* Vol.XXX, p.201.
14 *H.J.* Vol.XXIV, p.86.
15 *H.J.* Vol.XXVIII, p.102.
16 *H.J.* Vol.XIX, p.147.
17 *H.J.* Vol.XIII, p.54.
18 *H.J.* Vol.36, p.103.
19 *A.J.* Vol.LIX, p.288.
20 *H.J.* Vol.XX, p.104.
21 *H.J.* Vol.XXIII, p.56.
22 *H.J.* Vol.XXV, p.113.
23 *H.J.* Vol.XXIX, p.118.
24 *H.J.* Vol.XXXIII, p.129 and p.147; Vol.36, p.113; Vol.44, p.107.
25 *H.J.* Vol.39, p.69.
26 *H.J.* Vol.41, p.184.
27 *H.J.* Vol.XXX, p.228.
28 *H.J.* Vol.XXXIII, p.151.

68 SAFINA (5975 M)

Named after the celestial boat which transports its passengers to heaven (imagery popular in Balti philosophy), Safina is representative of the abundant climbing to be found amongst lesser peaks of the Eastern Karakoram. Rising above the junction of the North Terong glacier and the 'Sondhi' glacier, it was first climbed by an Indo-British team (Harish Kapadia) by its west ridge in 1985.

69 RIMO III (7233 M)

Located on the northern continuation of the ridge connecting Rimo I and Rimo II, this peak was first climbed by an Indo-British team in 1985 (Harish Kapadia). Two climbers crossed the Ibex col from the North Terong glacier and descended to the South Rimo glacier to gain the northeast ridge which was followed to the summit. No further attempts have been made on this mountain. The south face remains a tough challenge.

68 SAFINA *from North Terong glacier (Harish Kapadia).*

69 RIMO III, *south face (Harish Kapadia).*

SASER KANGRI MASSIF

Saser La

Skyangpoche

35° 0'

Tulum Puti Tokpo

West Chamshen Gal

East Chamshen Gal

Shyok Rvr

Sasoma

Cloud Peak
7415

North Phukpoche Gal

Saser Kangri
Plateau Peak
7310

IV

I

7672

III

7495

Nubra R

South Phukpoche Gal

Sakang
6750

North Shukpai Kunchang Gal

N

Panamik

Sakang Lungpa Gal

W 7518
II E
7518

Look Out
Peak 6252

0   5   10 KM

△ Heights in metres

KISHTWAR

6520

Sarbal Gal

Sickle
Moon
6574

Hagshu Gal

Eiger
6000
6013

West Donalli Gal

East Donalli Gal

Barnaj
6250
I
II
6170
6150
C
6290
S

Hagshu
La

Hagshu
6300

Brammah Gal

Chiring
6100

5279
Brammah
I 6416
5630
Crooked
Finger

West Donalli Gal

Barnaj Nala

Brammah
6425 II

Flat Top
6100

Umasi
La

Arjuna
6230

Machail

Bhujwas

Kishtwar
Shivling
6000

Sibshpahar
6040

Chisote

Laul
6139

Agyasol
6200

N

Dhariang R

Chenab R

6062
Mardi
Phabrang

0   5   10 KM

Atholi

△ Heights in metres

6
KISHTWAR

NESTLING ON THE northeast bank of the Chenab, between Kashmir to the north and Chamba-Lahul to the south, is the mountaineer's playground of Kishtwar.

The first mountaineers to visit Kishtwar were probably three Austrians who, after making the first ascent of Mulkila in Lahul in 1939, were interned in India at the outbreak of war. Eight years later in 1947, whilst waiting for their passages back home, Fritz Kolb, with his friends Ludwig Krenek and Fabian Geduldig, visited the Kishtwar range. From a base at Machail they explored the eastern approaches to Sickle Moon, the highest peak in the range, and climbed two small peaks. They considered making an alpine-style ascent of Agyasol from the north, but they decided to visit Zanskar instead. However, their first attempt to cross the main Himalayan watershed failed, when much to their surprise, the difficult Muni la led to the Dharlang nala. This not only confounded them, but has confused mapmakers ever since. They continued up the Dharlang nala and crossed the remote Poat la into Zanskar, and returned to the Kishtwar side over the Umasi la. Their time of three days for this arduous journey of nearly a hundred miles was remarkable. Six days is now considered normal for trekking parties travelling from Machail to Padam over the Umasi la.[1]

The area remained almost untouched for a further

eighteen years when Charles Clarke led two expeditions in 1965 and 1969. During his first visit (with the Cambridge University team) he explored the central glacier system and the Kiar nala and attempted Brammah I (6416 m). 1969 saw him return with a few British and Indian friends to explore the Brammah glacier and Kiar nala further. They made the first ascent of Crooked Finger (5630 m) lying on the ridge north of Flat Top (6100 m).[2]

Little is known of N. Clough's expedition of 1970 except that some more exploration of the Brammah area was made. In 1971, however, Charles Clarke returned once again with a British team for a serious attempt on Brammah I, and got to within a hundred metres of the summit. Deep loose snow lying on ice ready to avalanche warned them off further progress when all technical difficulties had been overcome. Rather than make another attempt, they chose to explore the highest peak in the area – Sickle Moon (6574 m).[3] Brammah I was first climbed by Nick Estcourt and Chris Bonington in 1973.[4] It was again climbed by the British (A. Wheaton) in 1978 but two members were lost in the process.

Rob Collister led a small British team to Brammah II (6425 m) in 1975, but failed to find a viable route.[5] They however consoled themselves by the ascent of Pk 5685 m (and predictably christened it Consolation Peak). While the British were scouting around the Donali glacier and the Kijai nala, a Japanese team (K. Keira) made the first ascent of Brammah II from the Brammah glacier (and Nanth nala)[6] on 15 September, 1975. Brammah II was merely marked Pk 6425 m before the climbers got to grips with it. The name was given much later and even though it is higher than Brammah I, it has gained currency, and the name has stuck.

Another Japanese expedition (F. Yuki) attempted Sickle Moon, before it finally allowed an Indian High-Altitude Warfare School expedition (Col D. N. Tanka) to make the first ascent. That was all in 1975.

The next year (1976) six teams visited Kishtwar. The rush had indeed started as the attractive challenges became more widely known. J. Cant led a British team which attempted Arjuna (6230 m) and made first ascents of 'Sher Khan', 'Taragiri' and 'Sundar Pahar' (all expedition names). Chris Bonington's team attempted Katori and there were three Japanese expeditions. One made the first ascent of Pk 6550 m (Doda Peak) above Durung Drung glacier from Abring in the Doda valley, another attempted Barnaj II (6290 m) and made the first ascent of Pk 5310 m nearby, and the third made yet another attempt on Sickle Moon. Finally a British expedition (A. Judkowski) attempted Cathedral (5370 m).

The avalanche of visits continued in the following years and between 1977 and 1985 a good number of the prominent peaks received their first ascent. (But let no one be disheartened, as there is still enough climbing left in Kishtwar for a number of generations of rock and ice specialists, as well as for the more modest in skill and technique). Prominent amongst the first ascents, and all in 1977, were those of Barnaj II (central and south summits) by the Japanese (N. Kubo); 'Viewpoint' (c.5600 m) and 'Delusion Peak' (6560 m – doubtful height, hence its name) by the British (R. Collister);[7] Gharol (c.6000 m) by the Indian Army Signals (Maj A. G. Roy). Brahmasar by the British (C. Graham); Pk 5750 m (named 'Maguclonne' by the team) south of Barnaj II by the British again (L. Griffin) in 1978; Brammah's Wife (5297 m) by the Poles (W. Fint); Pk 6013 m (east of Eiger), the Poles again (M. Kokaj), both in 1979. Flat Top (6100 m) was climbed first by the British (Maj R. Wilson) who were followed by the Italians led by A. Bergamaschi who climbed six peaks in the Durung Drung range in 1980.[7]

The preserve of the British and Japanese teams was now to be shared by the Poles, Italians, French and the Dutch. The British continued to outnumber the other nationalities both in the frequency of visits as well as the area of climbing/exploration. D. Hillebrant led the British Padar expedition to several ascents around the Hagshu and Umasi nalas. 1981 was no less remarkable for its first ascents of Agyasol (c.6200 m) and Spire Peak (c.5000 m) by the British (S. Richardson),[8] and the Polish first ascent of Arjuna South from the Kijai nala. New routes up already climbed peaks began to be attempted and the permutations and variety offered by this were endless. 1983 was a year of two spectacular first ascents – that of Kishtwar-Shivling by its north face by Stephen Venables and Dick Renshaw,[9] and the Polish (B. Slarno) success on Arjuna (6230 m) main summit. Another first ascent that year was 'La Shal' (6135 m) by the French (J-P. Chassagne). This peak is probably Chiring's south summit, since in 1987 Andy Dunhill and Roger Brooks, having failed on Hagshu, climbed Chiring South and found an abseil sling on its summit. (The I.M.F. recorded the French as having climbed Hagshu – the French having climbed from the Hagshu nala reinforced the error.)

The years 1984–7 have been no less active, where most of the expeditions have been exploring and attempting peaks, trying out alternate routes and in general consolidating the knowledge of the area. For instance, another fine piece of exploration-cum-ascent was that of a British team (S. Richardson) in 1984. After having been thwarted on the northeast pillar of 'Mardi Phabrang' by three weeks of continuous snowfall, most of the team returned to Delhi, while Richardson set off alone up the Kaban nala. The most prominent peaks are those of Tupendo I (*c.*5700 m) and II (*c.*5600 m) to its left. The latter is a snow peak (a rarity in Kishtwar), and Richardson crossed the Agyasol glacier, onto a col between the two peaks and climbed the broad south ridge to the summit. Richardson considers the northeast pillar of 'Mardi Phabrang', at the western end of the Agyasol group, one of the finest prizes in the area. His article in the *H.J.* Vol. 45 is full of tempting suggestions. In 1988 the inevitable ski descent was made down Brammah I's 1500 m face by the Swiss (N. C. Dominique). The intrepid Simon Richardson led yet another British team to a first ascent of Chomochior (6322 m) which lies between the Haptal and Chomochior glaciers. The British were also scrambling around Kalidahar (5835 m) which they climbed (Carl Schaske and Jeff Knight), ushering in an era of pure rock climbs to modest heights but far from modest difficulties. The rest of the team were as active; Conran Anker and Kevin Green climbed the north ridge of Kalidahar Spire (*c.*5600 m) by a superb fifteen-pitch route (5.10 and A2), but the Spire's northwest face resisted the attentions of

Geoff Hornby and Tom Norris.[10]

Kishtwar is the small party's hunting ground – there are innumerable valleys which are yet to be visited and the sheer variety of rock and ice formation is enough to satiate the most ardent alpinist, even if he ignored the prominent summits. All he has to do is to change into a higher gear of technique and into a lower gear of his ego (and mania for height records).

KISHTWAR REFERENCES

1 *H.J.* Vol.XIV, p.33.
2 *H.J.* Vol.XXX, p.237.
3 *H.J.* Vol.XXXI, p.250.
4 *H.J.* Vol.XXXIII, p.142.
5 *H.J.* Vol.XXXIV, p.88.
6 *H.J.* Vol.XXXV, p.278.

7 *H.J.* Vol.42, p.191.
8 *H.J.* Vol.39, p.79.
9 *H.J.* Vol.40, p.109 and
   Painted Mountains, Stephen
   Venables, London, 1986.
10 *H.J.* Vol.45, p.90.

70 RIMO I, *west face (Harish Kapadia).*

70 RIMO I (7385 M)
The highest of the group of the 'Painted Mountains', it dominates the divide between the North Terong-South Rimo glaciers. It was first attempted in 1985 by the Indo-British team (Harish Kapadia) by a route which got onto the southwest ridge by its southern slopes. A dropped rucksack at a crucial stage compelled retreat from a height of 6900 m. The first ascent was made in 1988 by an Indo-Japanese party (Hukam Singh) by its south face. A number of challenging routes comprise the west face, the southwest ridge and the east ridge.

7

KASHMIR, LADAKH AND ZANSKAR

KASHMIR

THE GREAT HIMALAYAN axis runs southeast from Nanga Parbat to Nun-Kun. This forms the northern boundary of Kashmir. Beyond this to the northeast lies Ladakh, to the east lies Zanskar and towards the southeast lies Kishtwar. They all form part of Kashmir as a state, but for mountaineers, they are different geographical entities.

The Sind river meets the Liddar in the broad vale of Kashmir and they both cut a gorge through the Pir Panjal range near Baramula, the Pir Panjal itself forming the southern boundary of the valley. There are some famous and important passes on both sides of Kashmir. On the Pir Panjal the best known is the Pir Panjal pass (3490 m) which gives its name to the whole mountain range. It was the most frequented pass between the Punjab and Kashmir and was in ancient times the one used by the Moghul Emperors. The other pass, Banihal (2740 m), has in current times been the common route into Kashmir. The Jhelum Cart-Road was constructed in the 1880s and a motor road was made through the pass in 1910 and metalled in 1922. Later, in the 1960s, a long tunnel through Banihal was engineered, which now allows vehicular traffic to ply throughout the year. To the north, the lowest notch in the range is the Zoji la (3530 m) which was the main caravan route to Leh and distant Central Asia. Genghis Khan is reported to have used this pass on one of his adventures. Now a metalled road leads tourists across it, but even so it is not all plain sailing. A freak storm killed eighty persons one evening in 1987. The other pass Bat Kol (or Lonvilad pass) is a deep notch at 4490 m between two peaks on the direct route from Jammu via the Warwan valley to Suru and Leh. It was used by the army of the Dogra General, Zorawar Singh, in 1834.

Today when one talks of Kashmir, the political realities have to be taken into account. Once, the State was the starting point for all the caravans, shikaris and climbers venturing into the Karakoram. In 1947 it became the bone of contention between India and Pakistan and has since then witnessed hostilities in 1962, 1965 and in 1971. One can now admire Nanga Parbat from Gulmarg but to reach its base (as for all the other peaks in the Western Karakoram) one has to pass through Pakistan. The mountains and valleys described in this volume are those confined to the Indian-held part of the original State.

In the valley of Kashmir, no summit rises above 6000 m but there are innumerable peaks between 4800–5800 m. They afford much pleasure, are interesting from the technical angle and most of them are easily accessible from Srinagar. The three main peaks that have drawn attention to themselves are Kolahoi (5425 m), Haramukh (5143 m) and Koh-i-Nur (5137 m).[1]

Two names stand out in the climbing history of the Kashmir valley, those of Drs Arthur and Ernest Neve. They came to Kashmir in 1882 and between them visited almost every valley in Kashmir. They climbed most of the higher summits of the Pir Panjal lying in Kashmir, as well as all the five summits of the Haramukh massif. Ernest visited and explored the Kolahoi area six times between 1900–10, and in 1912 made the first ascent with Kenneth Mason of the highest summit in the Kolahoi group. Mason, as editor of the *Himalayan Journal*, paid glowing tribute to the two brothers. 'No mountaineer who has visited Kashmir during the last half-century has ever appealed to our veteran member for advice and help in vain. Dr Ernest Neve joined his brother Arthur, who had been at the Mission Hospital in Srinagar for four years, in the winter of 1886. They learned to know and love the people and their land; they carried hope and health to every remote village in the State and, long before any Himalayan Club came into existence, they were the fountainheads of information to which all mountaineers went for advice.' Their articles in the *Himalayan Journal* and Ernest's book *Beyond the Pir Panjal* were the main references for all the early climbing in the State.[2]

The Surveyors, as in all the other ranges, were there well before the climbers. Capt T. G. Montgomerie was the chief organiser for the Survey of Kashmir. From Haramukh, in 1858, he saw the great mountains of the Karakoram for the first time. G. Shelverton took the first observations, and K2 was 'discovered' and measured.[3]

One of the major climbing areas is that of the Thajiwas glacier and its environs. There are innumerable peaks within easy reach of Sonamarg and Pahlgam. Wilfrid Noyce published for the Himalayan Club a most useful monograph describing the climbing prospects entitled *A Climber's Guide to Sonamarg*. It comprised the sum of the knowledge available at the time, compiled from the reports of the instructors of the Aircrew Mountain Centre at Sonamarg around 1944 who had actually made the various ascents. This little handbook, and a revision of it by John Jackson entitled *Sonamarg Climbing and Trekking Guide*, has done much to excite interest in the area and popularise the excellent small-scale climbs available.[4]

Let us return to the three major peaks of the Kashmir valley.

Kolahoi (5425 m)
This group of peaks, the highest of which is as noted above, were the main target for climbers in the early days.[5] It is locally known as 'Gashibrar' (the Goddess of Light). Its first recorded attempt was in 1911 by Capt Corry and Lt Squires. The same year Dr E. Neve and K. Mason made the first ascent of a lower peak to the south known as Bur Dalau (5110 m). In 1912, they returned, following the Armium Nar, crossing the Har Nag pass and climbed through what is now known as the 'Neve-Mason Couloir' to climb the main summit. The next ascent was by C. R. Cooke and Lt B. W. Battye in 1926. They climbed the east ridge via the Neve-Mason Couloir. Returning from their trip to the Karakoram

in 1935, John Hunt and Rowland Brotherhood followed a different route to the summit. Since then the mountain has been on the favourite list of many mountaineers and has received several ascents.[6] There are quite a number of smaller summits in the group which could offer a variety of technical challenges to those with a head for lesser heights.

Koh-i-Nur group
There are three peaks in this group. In 1898, C. G. Bruce climbed the northeastern summit whilst Karbir, one of his Gurkhas, made the first ascent of the southeast and highest peak (5137 m). The middle summit, Kunyirhayan (5098 m), was climbed in 1911 by Capt J. B. Corry, Lt R. D. Squires and K. Mason.[7]

Haramukh (5143 m)
This comprises a group of five peaks. The first recorded ascent of the main summit was by Dr E. Neve and G. W. Millais in 1899. This was followed by C. G. Bruce and A. L. Mumm in 1907, and since then has been regularly climbed, along with the other summits in the group.[8]

It is difficult to describe the beauty of Kashmir in mere words. Its *chinars*, pines, poplars, with its alps, lakes and mountains, have had their praises sung from time immemorial. Travellers, especially those returning from the drier parts of Ladakh and Zanskar, have been charmed by the contrast of the lush green vale. It is therefore not difficult to agree whole-heartedly with the famous Chinese traveller, Huen Tsang who, descending from Zoji la after a year of travel in Central Asia, looks down towards Sonamarg and says, 'If there is a paradise on earth, it is here, it is here, it is here . . .'

KASHMIR REFERENCES
1 *Abode of Snow*, Kenneth Mason, London, 1955.
2 *H.J.* Vol.XII, p.117.
3 *H.J.* Vol.XI, p.184; Vol.II, p.67.
4 *H.J.* Vol.VI, p.127; Vol.XIII, p.87.
5 *H.J.* Vol.XVI, p.112.
6 *H.J.* Vol.VIII, p.103; Vol.X, p.159.
7 *H.J.* Vol.II, p.66.
8 *H.J.* Vol.VII, p.148.

LADAKH

L ADAKH IS SOMETIMES called 'Little Tibet'. It has a similar landscape and culture that bears this comparison. It lies to the east-northeast of Kashmir and forms a part of the State. For many years, the caravans from Kashmir and Yarkand (in Central Asia) met in the bazars of Leh. The ethnic mixture can still be observed in its streets.

A motorable road and an airport now link Ladakh with the rest of Kashmir almost throughout the year. To its north lies the Khardung la, a motorable pass leading to the Eastern Karakoram (Nubra valley). The Ladakh range lies on this ridge pointing northwest-southeast. This is the watershed between the Shyok and the Indus rivers. Numerous peaks up to 6200 m are to be found on this ridge. None of them has been climbed or attempted, because of the tight security, as well as their unattractively low heights.

South of Leh is Zanskar, technically a part of Ladakh, but to the mountaineers it has a separate identity. To the east is the Pangong range which derives its name from the unique Pangong lake. This lake is more than 200 km long and on an average five km wide. Only about forty-five km of its L-shape is under Indian control, the rest of it being in Tibet. To the south of this lake is a group of mountains, the highest of which, Pk 6725 m, was climbed in 1988 by the I.T.B.P. (Illam Singh).[1] Only two more peaks in this area have been climbed – one of them is Kakshett (6442 m), the southernmost of the range which was climbed in 1973 by the I.T.B.P. With the Tibet border just across the shores of the lake, it will be a long long time before any civilian mountaineers are allowed here.

The Indus, originating in Western Tibet, flows northwest and enters Ladakh near Demchok and subsequently passes through Leh. This is the famous Rupshu district. There were a few early travellers, who came from Spiti which lies to its south. Two famous passes, the Parang la and the Takling la, lead into Rupshu from Spiti. To the south one finds several high peaks like Mata (6340 m), Monto (6230 m), Thalda Kurmi (6666 m), Zongchenmo (6470 m), along with a host of unnamed summits rising up to 6600 m. Except for Mata II (6277 m) (R. D. Bhattacharji) and the unnamed Pk 6428 m (I.T.B.P.) near Chumar, there has been hardly any serious mountaineering in this area.[2] The southern periphery of Ladakh here is enclosed by the Spiti peaks dominated by Gya (6794 m) and Parilungbi (6166 m) in the Lingti valley.

Rupshu stretches from the Tunglung la to the north, to Chumar in the south, Manecham Sump in the west and Hanle to the east, encompassing an area of about 15,000 sq km. It is an exceedingly dry district, even by Tibetan standards. All this expanse of high desert is nowhere below 4500 m. There are only three places where there are permanent dwellings. In 1984, as in 1881, the population comprised about 500 nomads who still live in tents of black hair-cloth. One of the two unique features of Rupshu is the Tso Morari, an oval shaped lake typical of the area and nestling between Mata and Monto. The other curiosity lies to the west. A huge ice-plateau almost 6000 m in average height. Pilots flying over it for their air drops have nick-named it the 'Rupshu Ice-cap'. It drains on one side into Rupshu and on the other west side into Zanskar. This ice-cap is in the Panpo Lungpa region of West Rupshu and consists of huge snowfields arranged steplike, rising from 4800–6100 m. The only known visit to a part of this ice-cap was by Gen Strachey in 1846 who observed that there were 'two large permanent snowfields in places 4 or 5 feet thick. They were 3 or 4 miles apart at an elevation of about 16,000 feet. The valley bottom was a mile wide, and exposed to the sun all day, and 2000 feet below the snow-line on the neighbouring mountains.' The snow-line in the eastern and drier part of this district is at 6100 m, whereas on the western side it can be as low as 5200 m. The Rupshu Ice-cap is indeed a real geographical curiosity. Any crossings or climbs on this plateau will be genuine exploration stuff, even in the present days of satellites.

LADAKH REFERENCES
1 *H.J.* Vol.45, pp.147–8.
2 *H.J.* Vol.41, p.82.

ZANSKAR

THE DISTRICT lying south of Ladakh receives its name from the river which flows north from Padam in Central Zanskar and which, with its many tributaries, finally joins the Indus a little west of Leh. It forms a terrific gorge and flows through vast plains. Zanskar has always been the most inhabited part of Ladakh, with several small villages which maintain close contacts with Kashmir, Lahul and Kishtwar – some recent claims to have 'discovered' Zanskar are that much wishful thinking.[1] It has many gompas, and trade routes criss-cross the area – to its south lies Kishtwar with its jagged peaks; the Shingo la in the southeast leads to Lahul whilst to the northwest is Kargil and the road to Kashmir. It is one of the more popular areas for the trekkers. For the climber there are some select areas also. Peaks rising south of Padam and all peaks bordering Kishtwar can be approached from Zanskar, but the chief attraction is of course Nun (7135 m) and Kun (7087 m).

Nun-Kun

This is the most important massif in the Kashmir Himalaya. Standing at the edge of the Zanskar mountains it is a group of high summits – Nun (7135 m), Kun (7087 m) and Pinnacle Peak (6952 m). The massif stands on the Great Himalayan Axis in line with Nanga Parbat and lies immediately south of Tongul at the bend of the Suru river which joins the Shingo tributary of the Indus about eight km below Kargil. Between Nun and Kun is a high snow-plateau ending in a broken icefall and then descending further to become the eastern branch of the Parchik glacier. The main branch of this glacier drains the west ridge of Nun. The southeastern slopes of Pinnacle Peak flow into the Shafat glacier and eventually into the Suru river. The southern slopes drain into the Fariabad river which passes south through Kishtwar.

In 1898, C. G. Bruce and Maj F. G. Lucas were the first climbers here. In 1902 and 1904, Dr Arthur Neve and Rev C. E. Barton came up the Shafat glacier and made some sketches of the area to correct the old inaccurate maps. The

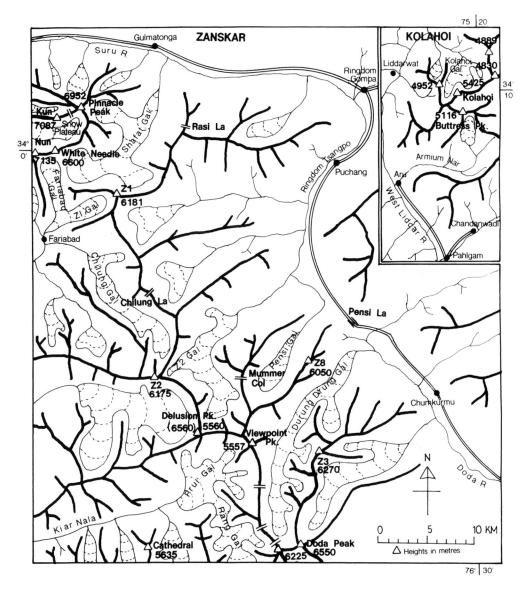

Dutch traveller, Dr H. Sillem, explored the high plateau between Nun and Kun in 1903 and was followed by the Americans, Dr and Mrs Bullock Workman, in 1906, who made some more surveys and climbed Pinnacle Peak. Dr Neve was back again in 1910 with Rev M. E. Wigram and climbed the neighbouring peak D41 on the ridge extending west from Nun.

The first ascent of Kun was by the Italian Count Piacenza, in 1913. His party climbed via its northeast ridge, approaching from the snow-plateau in the south.

Attempts on Nun continued. J. Waller tried the east ridge in 1934 and eventually climbed 'White Needle' (6599 m), immediately to the east of Nun. He returned in 1937 to try the west ridge. He was followed by R. Berry in 1946 and by the Swiss, P. Vittoz, in 1952. Finally P. Vittoz and Mme C. Kogan, members of a French expedition led by Bernard Pierre climbed Nun by the west ridge from the Fariabad valley in 1953.[2] All the major summits of the area have now been climbed. Today, Nun-Kun and the surrounding area have become perhaps the most visited and popular climbing arenas.

The second ascent of Nun was made in 1971 (Indian, K. P. Venugopal) by its east ridge. In 1975 a Swedish team climbed the west ridge again. The new routes on this peak are the northwest ridge (Czechs, 1976), west face (Austrians, 1980) and the north face (Americans, 1980). On the American expedition of 1980, Dr Thomas Mutch, a nuclear scientist, was benighted due to injury. He was anchored on a ledge, but when the party returned with help the next day, there was no trace of him.

Kun received its second and third ascents in 1971 and 1978, both by the Indian Army. The west wall of Kun was climbed by the Japanese in 1981 after a twelve-day ordeal. They reached the summit twice – on 5 July it was cloudy, so they returned the next day from their last bivouac to take photographs!

Both Nun and Kun have suffered skiers, Sylvia Saudan on Nun in 1977 and the Indian Army on Kun in 1978. Now they are being climbed with monotonous regularity by the various routes and both qualify for the title of the 'most oft-climbed seven-thousanders'.

Peaks in Zanskar near Nun-Kun are numbered with a prefix 'Z'. These peaks lie on the periphery of the Durung Drung glacier, and have become an important climbing region in Zanskar, which offers plenty of excellent prospects. Its best climbs are yet to come. The Z group of peaks have been visited only in recent years. The exception to this is Z3 (6270 m) which was climbed by Piacenza of the Italian expedition in 1913.[3] The second ascent was made sixty-eight years later, in 1981, by another Italian expedition (G. Agostoni).

Z1 (6181 m) was climbed by the Japanese (M. Ouchi) by its southwest ridge, Z2 (6175 m) by the Italians in 1977 by its south ridge. They came over a high pass from the Pensi glacier into the Rumdum glacier. Earlier they had climbed Z8 (6050 m) by its northwest ridge from the Pensi glacier. All these were first ascents. In fact, due to publication of an Italian pictorial book of this area after the first ascent of Kun in 1914, it has become a very popular hunting ground for the Italians, closely followed by the Japanese who have also climbed a number of unnamed summits. Because of the paucity of accurate maps, it is difficult to trace all these fine ascents with any degree of exactitude. The rush is bound to come soon – the easy approach and the multitude of six-thousanders cannot possibly lie unnoticed for long.

A number of parties have, in the last few years, visited the mountains at the head of the Durung Drung glacier. It flows north and slightly east from the Kishtwar-Zanskar water-shed towards the Pensi la. The British and the Italians have been particularly active. In 1977, G. Cohen, R. Collister and D. Rubens made some serious climbs. Returning in 1983, G. Cohen with C. Huntley made some more ascents. Geoff Cohen in particular has been responsible for opening up the area to knowledge with the help of whatever inaccurate maps are available. Two Italian expeditions, A. Bergamaschi in 1980 and G. Agostino in 1981, climbed several peaks in the area, giving Italian names and heights by altimeter. Amongst other visitors were those from the Edinburgh University (1983), Alan Hunt (1983), Joss Lynam (1983) and K. Sakai with a Japanese party (1985). The Z series of summits have certainly not seen the last of the climbers yet.

ZANSKAR REFERENCES
1 *Zanskar, The Hidden Kingdom*, Michel Peissel, London, 1979.
2 *A Mountain Called Nun Kun*, Bernard Pierre, London, 1955.
3 *H.J.* Vol.42, p.191; Vol.43, p.146.

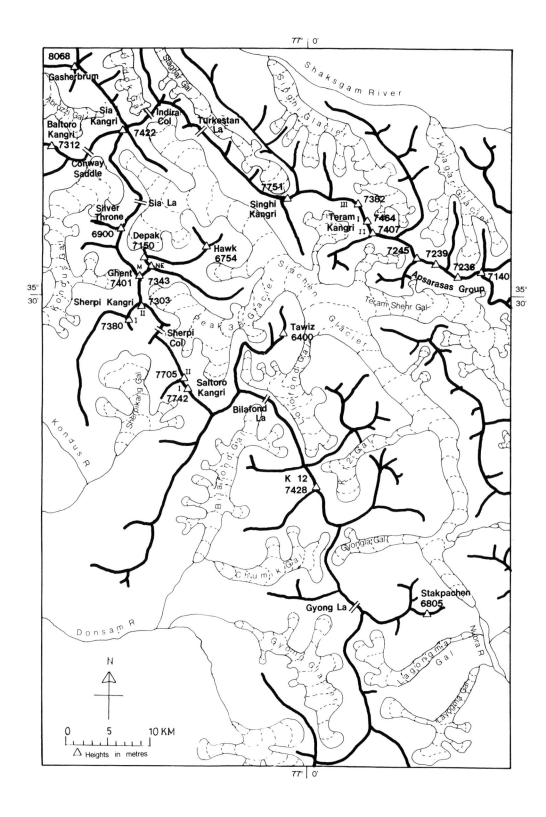

77° | 0'

8068
Gasherbrum

Abruzzi Gal

Sia Kangri

Staghar Gal

Siaghi Glacier

Shaksgam River

Indira Col

Turkestan La

Baltoro Kangri
△ 7312

7422

Conway Saddle

Silver Throne
△ 6900

Sia La

Singhi Kangri

7751

Kyagar Glacier

III △ 7382
Teram Kangri
I 7464
II 7407

Depak
7150

Hawk
6754

Siachen Glacier

7245

7239
7236

Apsarasas Group
7140

Kondus Gal

Ghent
7401

M
7343 NE

35° 30'

Sherpi Kangri

7303

II
7380 I

Peak 36

Teram Shehr Gal

35° 30'

Sherpi Col

Sherpikang Gal

Tawiz
6400

Lolofond Glacier

Lolofond Gal

7705 II
7742 I
Saltoro Kangri

Bilafond La

Bilafond Gal

Kondus R

K 2 Gal

K 12
7428

Gyongla Gal

Chumik Gla

Stakpachen
6805

Gyong La

Donsam R

N

Gyong Gla

Lagong ma Gal

Nubra R

Layoong pa Gal

0   5   10 KM

△ Heights in metres

77° | 0'

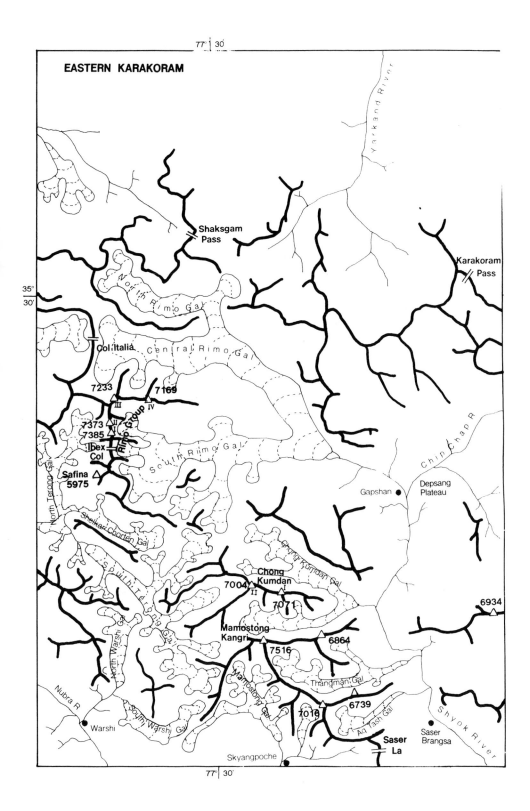

EASTERN KARAKORAM

77° 30'

Yarkand River

Shaksgam
Pass

Karakoram
Pass

35°
30'

North Rimo Gal

Col Italia   Central Rimo Gal

7233   7169
      III
         IV
Rimo Group
7373 II
7385 I
Ibex
Col
South Rimo Gal
Safina
5975

North Terong Gal

Chip Chap R

Gapshan ●   Depsang
                 Plateau

Shelkar Chorten Gal

Chong Kumdan Gal

South Terong Gal

Chong
Kumdan
7004   II
    7071

North Warshi Gal

Mamostong
Kangri
6864
7516   6934

Nubra R

South Warshi Gal

Mamostong Gal

Thangman Gal

7010   6739

Shyok River

Warshi ●

Aq Tash Gal

Skyangpoche ●

Saser
La

Saser
Brangsa ●

77° 30'

8
EASTERN
KARAKORAM

THIS AREA which has been reopened only recently to the mountaineering fraternity offers ample scope for exploration as well as climbing. The Eastern Karakoram comprises the Siachen Muztagh, the Rimo Muztagh and the Saser Muztagh – all being sub-groups of the Great Karakoram range. Muztagh (*Muz*, ice; *tagh*, mountain) is a name given to almost all great snow-capped mountains by the Turki traders. The Muztaghs (or sections of the Karakoram range) are identified by the long glaciers which drain the mountain groups, each named where possible from its chief summit, and includes several satellites. The various groups, their subgroups and the individual peaks are well classified in the Karakoram Conference Report of 1936.[1]

Siachen Muztagh has had a fairly long and varied record of exploration, dating as far back as 1821 when W. Moorcroft passed near the snout of the glacier and first reported its existence.[2] G. T. Vigne attempted to reach the Bilafond la in 1835 from the west, never guessing that such a gigantic glacier lay across the pass.[3] H. Strachey was the first actually to step on to the 'Siachar' glacier in 1848, and walked two miles up it from its snout along the Nubra valley.[4] Dr T. Thompson in the same year[5] and F. Drew a year later[6] also managed to reach the glacier. E. C. Ryall of the Survey of India sketched the lower part of the glacier in 1861, but surprisingly estimated its length as a mere sixteen miles. It was Sir Francis Younghusband who set matters right during

his second journey to the Karakoram in 1889.[7] Approaching
from the Urdok valley in the north, he surveyed the massive
glacier from the Turkestan la and deduced that this was the
main axis of the Karakoram range, which indeed it was, and
which was later confirmed by Dr T. G. Longstaff in 1909.[8]
Dr Longstaff, along with Dr A. Neve and Lt Slingsby, were
the first to traverse the length and breadth of the Siachen
glacier. Initially they came over the Bilafond la (Saltoro
pass, as Longstaff named it) and named the glacier on the
opposite bank of Siachen, facing the pass, the 'Teram
Shehr' glacier, and the peaks along it the Teram Kangri
(group), after a Yarkandi legend. He returned over the pass
he had come by and came up again through the Nubra
valley, to establish the size of the Siachen up to the Turkestan la, its northern limit.

On his first views of Teram Kangri he made an estimation
of its height as being about 25,000 ft, but when his compass
and clinometer observations were calculated later there was
great excitement when the figure emerged at nearly 30,000
ft. It was of course realised that his angles and base were
such as to magnify the slightest deviation. His gut feeling of
25,000 ft was pretty close to the more careful and detailed
survey subsequently made in 1911 by V. D. B. Collins and
C. S. McInnes of the Survey of India[9] when Teram Kangri I
was evaluated at 24,489 ft (7464 m), Teram Kangri II at
24,300 ft (7407 m) and Teram Kangri III at 24,218 ft (7382
m).

The Bullock Workmans were the next explorers of note
and during 1911–12 they entered the Siachen glacier across
the Bilafond la, explored the Teram Shehr effluent, observed previously by Longstaff, and reached the two cols to
the north – 'Turkestan' and 'Indira' cols.[10] (The latter must
not be connected in any way with India's late Prime Minister, Mrs Indira Gandhi. The Workmans had named the col
in 1912 after the goddess Laxmi.) After a fairly detailed
survey of the Siachen supervised by Grant Peterkin and the
surveyors loaned to the expedition by the Survey of India,
the party withdrew over Sia la into the Kondus valley and
made a rapid survey of the southern flank of Baltoro Kangri
('Golden Throne'). This final bit of exploration enabled the

Survey of India to fix the heights and position of all the prominent peaks along the Shaksgam watershed.

An Italian expedition led by the Duke of Spoleto in 1929[11] explored a considerable area of the Karakoram. Amongst other explorations, they attempted to cross Indira col but were beaten back by bad weather. The glacier descending into the Urdok valley from the Turkestan la was named Staghar (Many Coloured). Another glacier descending the northern slopes of Teram Kangri was named (by the Balti porters) the Singhi (Difficult).

The years 1929 and 1930 saw Dr Ph. C. Visser and his wife make their third journey of exploration to the Karakoram.[12] Maj M. L. A. Gompertz, who in 1926 had surveyed the Mamostong glacier in the vicinity of Saser la, suspected the existence of a large unknown glacier system which flowed into the Nubra. Longstaff was more specific when he wrote, 'When it is desired to survey this unknown corner, will the party please proceed five miles up the Siachen glacier and take the first turning to the right.'[13] The Vissers followed this up and discovered the two Terong glaciers and the Shelkar Chorten glacier, which were totally unknown till then. The able surveyor Khan Sahib Afraz Gul, loaned to them by the Survey of India, mapped the area and thus completed the survey of the lower part of this great glacier.

Also in 1930 Prof Giotto Dainelli[14] who had been the geographer on the 1913–14 expedition of Filippo de Filippi, entered the Siachen in June, before the Nubra rose sufficiently to stop him. He spent two months on the glacier, establishing his base at the junction of Teram Shehr glacier. He then returned over a 6000 m pass, which he named 'Col Italia', into the Rimo glacier system which had been surveyed on the de Filippi expedition of 1914. This last exploration completed the survey of the Siachen in its major aspects.

Rimo Muztagh has had relatively few visitors and has been explored mainly by expeditions to the Siachen and adjacent areas. Initially it had been sketched by Johnson in 1864 and Shaw in 1869. One of the largest and most comprehensive scientific expeditions before the first world war was that of the Italian, Filippo de Filippi, during 1914.[15] It included geodesy, geophysics, geology, meteorology and climatology. For the survey, a detachment of the Survey of India under Major H. Wood was expanded by O. Marinelli, C. Alessandri and A. J. Spranger who came out from Europe.

Wood and the topographers made a complete survey of the Depsang plateau based on triangulation and fixed a number of new peaks to the west for subsequent exploration of the Rimo glacier. A. Alessio fixed additional points by triangulations, and the whole of the Rimo and its feeders were accurately mapped to connect with Peterkin's Siachen survey of 1912.

Saser Muztagh was first reconnoitred by Arthur Neve in 1899 followed by Longstaff in 1909 and Visser in 1922 and 1935. The main exploration was carried out by J. O. M. Roberts in 1946 when all the Saser peaks and their surrounding areas were covered. G. Lorimer who accompanied him also explored the northeastern side from the Chamshen tributary of the upper Shyok which he reached over the Saser la. Other groups in this Muztagh have yet to be visited.

Serious climbing activity in this part of the Karakoram perhaps started with Prof G. O. Dyhrenfurth's international expedition of 1934.[16] Although their main activity was in the Baltoro glacier, filming and photographing extensively, they set up a camp on the Conway Saddle which enabled them to be within striking distance of the east, west, central and main summits of Sia Kangri (7422 m), then known as Queen Mary Peak, named by the Bullock Workmans in 1912, but renamed to the present nomenclature at the Conference on Karakoram Nomenclature in 1936.

But let us start our climbing review from the eastern (and southern) aspect of our area under study, and proceed anti-clockwise.

The massive hulk of the Saser Kangri group lies at the heart of the loop of the mighty Shyok. One can approach it from the Nubra valley to its west or from the turbulent Shyok to its east. Both ways the approach tests the endurance of the party by the numerous river crossings it entails. The Nubra (a Shyok tributary) being a little more fordable has been preferred in most of the earlier attempts. Thus J. O. M. Roberts in his 1946 survey[17] came up the Nubra and faced the impossible west face of the mountain. No chink appeared and so as to leave no stone unturned, he crossed over a high saddle separating the Sakang Lungpa and the North Shukpa Kunchang glaciers to inspect feasibility from the eastern aspect. His report has been of considerable assistance to the expeditions that followed.

It is significant that the two Indian expeditions[18,19] that chose the Nubra approach failed to penetrate the western wall of the mountain. 'Look-out Peak' (6252 m) and some other smaller peaks in the area have been climbed as consolation, but the main summit, Saser I (7672 m), eventually allowed its first ascent from the long and arduous passage up the Shyok and from its eastern flank. The several crossings of the Shyok have been described as equally dangerous and soul-destroying as the windswept ridges on the mountain. The I.T.B.P. team (Cdr Joginder Singh, I. N.)[20] wormed its way up the North Shukpa Kunchang glacier, and pressed on to a col which fell steeply on the other side to the South Phukpoche and thence to the top (5, 6 and 7 June, 1973). This was the highest first ascent by an Indian team to date.

For the second ascent, the same route was used in 1979[21] by the Army (Col Jagjit Singh), but the 1987 ascent (third) by the Indo-British Armies team managed to gain the northwest ridge and not only climb the main summit, but also Saser IV (Cloud Peak) (7415 m).

Meanwhile in 1985 an Indo-Japanese expedition approached Saser Kangri II West (7518 m),[22] by the Nubra and up to the col between Saser II and III, making its ascent by the northwest ridge. A year later Saser III (7495 m) was climbed for the first time by its eastern flank, up the face and onto a col on the ridge between Plateau Peak (7310 m) and the summit. S. P. Chamoli led the I.T.B.P. on this fine effort.[23]

So it seems that the difficulty in negotiating the Shyok (not forgetting its spate, by the time the team is ready to return, and the consequent possibility of being marooned till autumn) is rewarded by the more accessible routes up the Saser massif.

As always, the logistics are heavily dependent on the degree of assistance that the local Army positions can offer. The remoteness and the almost total isolation from human habitation for miles around forces the mountaineer to plan to the last detail. In as highly sensitive an area as that of the Eastern Karakoram most expeditions are either of the Armed Forces or jointly sponsored by the I.M.F. and foreign clubs.

Let us continue our survey of the area. The next high prominence is Mamostong Kangri (7516 m), connected to the Saser peaks by a lengthy ridge studded with numerous six-thousanders and the Saser la which connects the Nubra valley with that of Shyok in the east. The Saser la has been traversed several times from the earliest days of exploration, and has even been used as an escape route from the enraged Shyok in full flood. Here again, although the Nubra approach was chosen by Col B. S. Sandhu, leading the Indo-Japanese team, the route crossed over a col into the Thangman glacier and climbed to the summit by its east ridge in 1984, thus further emphasising the formidable obstacle offered by the western approach to this chain of peaks.[24] In 1988 an Army team (Maj A. M. Sethi) crossed over the Saser la to enter the Thangman glacier from the east and the route of the first ascent was followed to the top.

West and north of Mamostong Kangri lies a complex mountain area which was visited early in the history of exploration, but hardly saw any mountaineers. The Rimo and Terong peaks form one of the most interesting climbing arenas in the Eastern Karakoram. Rimo IV (7169 m) was the first of the Rimo group to be climbed, in 1984 by the Indian Army (K. S. Sooch) who approached the massif from the east (Shyok valley and the Depsang plains). The paucity of visits was somewhat corrected by an I.M.F.-Alpine Club team (Harish Kapadia) in 1985.[25] The main target, no doubt, was Rimo I (7385 m), which eluded them, but they made the first ascent of Rimo III (7233 m). The North and South Terong and the Shelkar Chorten glaciers were well scoured by pairs of climbers who made eight first ascents, two attempts (including Rimo I) and the ascent and crossing of several interconnecting cols. A fine piece of work which has opened up great possibilities for the future. The following year (1986), a particularly incompatible Indo-Australian team (Col Prem Chand) attempted Rimo I by the south face and the east ridge. It was defeated as much by the dissension amongst the members as by bad weather and time limitations.[26]

The first ascent of Rimo I was made by an Indo-Japanese team (Hukam Singh), during July/August of 1988. From the North Terong glacier they crossed the Ibex Col and followed a couloir leading to the hanging glacier close to the summit which was reached via the south face. Two thousand metres of fixed rope above the Ibex Col enabled twelve members to get to the top.[27]

North of the Rimo group lies the unvisited Teram Shehr group, but moving westwards and adjoining the Siachen lie the chain of Teram Kangri and the Apsarasas peaks. The base camp for this massif lies at the obvious junction of the Siachen, Teram Shehr and the Lolofond glaciers. The first ascents of Teram Kangri I (7462 m) and Teram II (7407 m) were made by the Japanese in 1975[28] by the southwest ridge of Teram Kangri II, over its summit and continuing up to the main peak. Teram Kangri II was climbed for the second time in 1978 by the Indian Army (Col N. Kumar), not the first ascent, as claimed in the *H.J.* Vol. 37, p. 107, and has seen a few more attempts by the Army. Teram Kangri III (7382 m) was climbed by a Japanese team in 1979[29] by the same approach as the previous Japanese expedition to Teram II. Choosing the south ridge, they gained the arête connecting Teram III with Teram I and thence went to the top.

The Apsarasas, lying further east and up the Teram Shehr glacier, are really a continuation of the Teram chain. The first ascent of Apsarasas I (7245 m) by the Japanese in 1976[30] was by its south and western approach, over its south peak and further up the south ridge to the summit. The second[31] and the third ascents by the Indian Army also gained the summit via the south ridge in 1980 and in 1988.

Towards the eastern bank of the Siachen in the north lies

the Singhi group, containing the cirque that comprises the Turkestan la and the Indira col, with the Sia Kangri group forming the western bank of the glacier.

The single ascent of Singhi Kangri (7751 m) was made by the Japanese in 1976[32] who crossed over the wall dividing the Siachen from the Staghar glacier, where they sited their C2, and climbed along the northwest ridge to the summit.

The Sia group lies at the junction of the Siachen and the Abruzzi glacier (an offshoot of the famous Baltoro). The Sia la and the Conway Saddle separate the two mighty glacier systems. It is to be noted that for all its ascents Sia Kangri (7422 m) has been approached from the Conway Saddle and the western aspect of its south ridge: by the international expedition (Prof G. O. Dyhrenfurth) in 1934, the Austrians (Fritz Moravec) in 1956,[33] the Austrians again (Wolfgang Stefan) in 1974,[34] the Indians (Col N. Kumar) in 1981,[35] and an Indo-American team (Maj K. V. Cherian) in 1986.[36] This last ascent was made by the Indian contingent with the Pakistani gun positions a mere 600 m below them – apparently a combination of brinkmanship on the one hand, and gallant restraint on the other!

Below the Sia group, in the northwestern corner of the Siachen, lies the Kondus group comprising the Silver Throne (c.6900 m), Ghent (7401 m) with its northeast peak (7343 m) and its northern outlier Depak (7150 m). Here again all the ascents in this group have been via the Kondus glacier, but the route chosen is over the Sia la and onto the northern aspect of the massif, thence onto the northeast ridge on which lies not only the main summit of Ghent, but also Ghent Northeast and Depak.

Silver Throne on its west and a host of smaller satellites to the east have also been climbed from the Siachen side, after the main approach and base has been sited on the Kondus.

Ghent's first ascent was by the Austrians (E. Waschak) in 1961[37] who also climbed Silver Throne. The Austrian Alpine Club celebrated its Golden Jubilee by an expedition (B. Klausbruckner) in 1977[38] with the first ascent of Ghent Northeast, the second ascent of Depak and almost all the satellite six-thousanders in the area – a wonderful way to celebrate fifty years of the O.A.C. climbing group. In the following year, Ghent Northeast received its second ascent by the Japanese (H. Kobayashi)[39] and Ghent main summit also its second baptism by a German team (B. Scherzer) in 1980.[40]

Directly below the Kondus group and slightly off the main Siachen glacier – actually at the head of the Pk 36 glacier, a western tributary of Siachen – lies the Saltoro massif, comprising Sherpi Kangri (7380 m), Saltoro Kangri (7742 m) and Saltoro II (7705 m). Tawiz (c.6400 m) lies half-way down Pk 36 glacier between the Siachen and the Saltoro peaks.

It was in 1935[41] that exploratory work on the Saltoro Kangri was done by a team of British friends comprising John Hunt, J. Waller, Dr J. S. Carslaw and R. Brotherhood, who approached their target from the south over the Sherpikang and its tributary, the Lika glacier. They crossed over a saddle onto the Pk 36 glacier and made a brave attempt from the southeastern aspect. The final bit of the route can also be approached from the Pk 36 glacier and the usefulness of this discovery enabled all the subsequent ascents to be made thus. The first ascent of Saltoro Kangri by a Japanese–Pakistani expedition (Prof T. Shidei) in 1962[42] traversed the Bilafond over its pass into the Siachen and thence onto the Pk 36 glacier and used the very route pioneered by Hunt's party. Although another Japanese–Pakistani expedition (K. Namikawa) using the same route was foiled by bad weather in 1975,[43] the High-Altitude Warfare School team (Col N. Kumar) in 1981 again succeeded by the Hunt route. Saltoro II is still unclimbed and the only attempt by the Germans (G. Schultz) in 1976[44] was beaten back by a porters' strike and dangerous snow conditions made worse by the weather.

Sherpi Kangri from the south (via the Sherpikang glacier) is also a formidable proposition. It beat back two attempts, the first by the Japanese (T. Tanaka) in 1974[45] and then a British one (D. Alcock) the following year[46] by the terrifying aspect of its south face and the approach to any ridge that could possibly lead to the top. But a Japanese team (Prof K. Hirai) in 1976[47] had done their homework well. They opted for the west ridge which was gained with much danger and difficulty and with some lucky breaks in the weather made the first and only ascent to date.

Lying between the Bilafond and the Siachen glaciers is a maze of mountains, dominated by K12 (7428 m). Both approaches are possible – via Bilafond's tributary, the Grachma (Grachmolumba) glacier, or by Siachen's tributary, the K12 glacier. The Japanese (G. Iwatsubo) in 1974[48] used the former approach and made the first ascent, but alas the two summitters fell and disappeared during the descent. Another Japanese team (Y. Yamamoto) used the identical route the following year.[49] The Indian pre-Everest team (Col Premchand) in 1984[50] however used the Siachen-K12 glacier approach and followed the west ridge to its summit.

Earlier, an excellent piece of survey work, interspersed with climbs of smaller peaks, was carried out by the Imperial College Karakoram expedition in 1957, led by Eric Shipton. The area covered was around the Bilafond la and some interesting approaches to K12 were investigated.[51]

Much awaits the climber, and almost any glacier junction can be the source of good climbing fun. The main problem is that of getting there, but one's perseverance is well rewarded.

EASTERN KARAKORAM REFERENCES
 1 *H.J.* Vol.X, p.90.
 2 *Travels in Himalaya*, Moorcroft and Trebeck, London, 1841.
 3 *Travels in Kashmir*, G. T. Vigne, Vol.II, p.382, London, 1852.
 4 *Journal of the Royal Geographical Society* Vol.XXIII (1853).
 5 *Travels in Tibet*, Dr T. Thompson, London, 1924.
 6 *Jummoo and Kashmir Territories*, F. Drew, London, 1875.
 7 *Wonders of Himalaya*, Sir Francis Younghusband, London, 1924.
 8 *This My Voyage*, Dr T. G. Longstaff, London, 1950.
 9 *Abode of Snow*, Kenneth Mason, p.139, London, 1987.
10 *Two Summers in the Ice-Wilds of Eastern Karakoram*, Fanny B. Workman, London, 1917.
11 *H.J.* Vol.III, p.102.
12 *H.J.* Vol.III, p.13 – see also H. Osmaston's article in *H.J.* Vol.42, p.87.
13 *Abode of Snow*, Kenneth Mason, p.242, London, 1987.
14 *H.J.* Vol.IV, p.46.
15 *Himalaya, Karakoram and East Turkestan 1913–14*, G. Filippo de Filippi.
16 *H.J.* Vol.VII, p.142.
17 *H.J.* Vol.XIV, p.9.
18 *H.J.* Vol.XXV, p.136.

19 *H.J.* Vol.XXX, p.244.
20 *H.J.* Vol.XXXIII, p.119.
21 *H.C.N.L.* 33, p.22.
22 *H.J.* Vol.42, p.97.
23 *H.J.* Vol.43, p.84.
24 *H.J.* Vol.41, p.93.
25 *H.J.* Vol.42, p.68 – see also *Painted Mountains*, Stephen Venables, London, 1986.
26 *Rimo*, Peter Hillary, London, 1988.
27 *H.J.* Vol.45, p.104.
28 *H.C.N.L.* 31, p.17.
29 *H.C.N.L.* 33, p.23.
30 *H.C.N.L.* 32, p.20.
31 *H.J.* Vol.38, p.124.
32 *H.C.N.L.* 32, p.19.
33 *H.J.* Vol.XX, p.27 and corrections in *H.J.* Vol.XXI, p.137.
34 *H.C.N.L.* 31, p.5.
35 *H.J.* Vol.39, p.104.
36 *H.J.* Vol.43, p.80.
37 *H.J.* Vol.XXIII, p.47.
38 *H.C.N.L.* 32, p.34.
39 *H.C.N.L.* 33, p.7.
40 *H.C.N.L.* 34, p.25.
41 *H.J.* Vol.VIII, p.14.
42 *H.J.* Vol.XXV, p.143.
43 *H.C.N.L.* 31, p.17.
44 *H.C.N.L.* 32, p.19.
45 *H.C.N.L.* 31, p.4.
46 *H.C.N.L.* 31, p.18.
47 *H.J.* Vol.XXXV, p.254.
48 *H.C.N.L.* 31, p.4.
49 *H.C.N.L.* 31, p.16.
50 *H.J.* Vol.41, p.90.
51 *H.J.* Vol.XXI, p.33.

71 K12 (7428 m)

A high peak rising on the west of the Siachen glacier south of the Bilafond la. It was noticed by E. Shipton in 1957 and attempted in 1960 and 1971. The first ascent was made by the Japanese (G. Iwatsubo) in 1974. Two summitters radioed the news of their success but never returned. The peak was climbed again by the Japanese (Y. Yamamoto) in 1975. In 1984 it was climbed by the Indian Army from the Siachen glacier (Col Prem Chand).

72 SASER KANGRI I (7672 m)

Situated on the watershed of the Nubra and the Shyok, the Yellow Mountain was well surveyed by a British team (J. O. M. Roberts) in 1946. After an unsuccessful foray up the South Phukpoche glacier off the Nubra valley, they studied different sides of the mountain and noted that the north ridge offered a possible route. In 1956, an Indian team (Maj Nandu Jayal) crossed the South Phukpoche glacier and attempted to reach the South Col but abandoned the climb due to objective dangers. A later Indian expedition (Maj H. V. Bahuguna) similarly abandoned their attempt from the South Phukpoche glacier but made a circuitous attempt from the North Phukpoche glacier, climbing over Pk 6553 m and Pk 6858 m. They could not continue their southward traverse to bypass Saser IV (7446 m), as planned, and reach Saser Kangri I. The first ascent was made by an I.T.B.P. team (Cdr Joginder Singh) in 1973. They chose the Shyok approach, crossing the 32 km long North Shukpa Kunchang glacier, having made thirty-three river crossings en route to base. A determined effort up the south face was successful. Col Jagjit Singh led the Indian Army in 1979 to its second ascent. In 1987, the third ascent was made by an Indo-British Armies team (Col D. K. Khullar), from the Nubra valley, and following the northwest ridge.

71 K12, *east face (Stephen Venables).*

72 SASER KANGRI I, *west face (Harish Kapadia).*

SELECT BIBLIOGRAPHY

GENERAL

Aitkinson, E. T.: *The Himalayan Gazetteer*, Govt of India, Allahabad, 1882.
Bauer, Paul: *Kangchenjunga Challenge*, William Kimber, London, 1955.
Bauer, Paul: *Himalayan Quest*, Nicholson & Watson, London, 1938.
Braham, T.: *Himalayan Odyssey*, George, Allen & Unwin, London, 1974.
Bruce, C. G.: *Twenty Years in the Himalaya*, Arnold, London, 1910.
Gibson, J. T. M.: *As I Saw It*, Mukul Prakashan, Delhi, 1976.
Hunt, John: *Life is Meeting*, Hodder & Stoughton, London, 1978.
Longstaff, T. G.: *This My Voyage*, John Murray, London, 1950.
Mason, Kenneth: *Abode of Snow*, Rupert Hart Davis, London, 1955.
Mumm, A. L.: *Five Months in the Himalaya*, Arnold, London, 1909.
Noyce, Wilfrid: *Mountains and Men*, G. Bles, London, 1954.
Sircar, Joydeep: *Himalayan Handbook*, Private, Calcutta, 1979.
Wilson, Andrew: *The Abode of Snow*, Ratna Pastak Bhandar, (reprint)
    1979 (first published 1885, London).

SIKKIM AND ASSAM

Brown, Percy: *Tours in Sikkim*, W. Newman, Calcutta, 1934.
Cooke, C. R.: *Dust and Snow*, Private, London, 1988.
Freshfield, D. W.: *Round Kangchenjunga*, Arnold, London, 1903.
Kumar, Col N.: *Kangchenjunga*, Vision Books, New Delhi, 1978.
Waddell, A.: *Among the Himalayas*, Constable, London, 1899.

KUMAON AND GARHWAL

Boardman, Peter: *The Shining Mountain*, Hodder & Stoughton,
    London, 1978.
Bonington, C. J. S.: *Changabang*, Heinemann, London, 1975.
Calvert, H.: *Smythe's Mountains*, Victor Gollancz, London, 1985.
Gansser, A., Arnold, H.: *The Throne of the Gods*, Macmillan, London, 1939.
Kumar, Col N.: *Nilkantha*, Vision Books, New Delhi, 1965.
Languepin, J. J.: *Nanda Devi 1951*, Arthaud, Paris, 1952.
Murray, W. H.: *The Scottish Himalayan Expedition*, J. M. Dent & Son,
    London, 1957.
Patel, J.: *The Garhwal Kumaon Himalayas*, Himalayan Club, Bombay, 1985.
Randhawa, M. S.: *The Kumaon Himalayas*, Oxford and I.B.H., New
    Delhi, 1970.
Roskelley, J.: *Nanda Devi – the Tragic Expedition*, Stackpole Books,
    Harrisburg, 1987.
Smythe, F. S.: *Valley of Flowers*, Hodder & Stoughton, London, 1938.
Smythe, F. S.: *Kamet Conquered*, Victor Gollancz, London, 1932.
Shipton, Eric: *Nanda Devi*, Hodder & Stoughton, 1936.
Shipton, Eric: *That Untravelled World*, Hodder & Stoughton, London, 1969.
Singh, Jodh: *Himalayan Travels*.
Tilman, H. W.: *Ascent of Nanda Devi*, University Press, Cambridge, 1937.
Weir, Thomas: *The Ultimate Mountains*, Cassell, London, 1953.

KINNAUR

Kumar, K. I.: *Kinner Kailash Expedition*, Vision Books, New Delhi, 1979.
Mamgin, M. D.: *Kinnaur District Gazetteer*.
Pallis, Marco: *Peaks and Lamas*, Cassell, London, 1939.

SPITI
Holmes, Peter: *Mountains and a Monastery*, G. Bles, London, 1958.
Khosla, G. D.: *Himalayan Circuit*, Macmillan, London, 1956.

KULU AND LAHUL
Bruce, C. G.: *Kulu and Lahoul*, Arnold, London, 1914.
Bruce, C. G.: *Himalayan Wanderer*, Maclehose, London, 1934.
Chetwode, Penelope: *Kulu*, Allied Pub., Delhi, 1984.
Gill, M. S.: *Himalayan Wonderland*, Vikas Pub. Hse., Delhi, 1972.
Harcourt, A. F. P.: *The Himalayan Districts of Kooloo, Lahoul and Spiti*,
    Vivek Pub. Hse, (reprint) 1972.
Khosla, G. D.: *Himalayan Circuit*, Macmillan, London, 1956.
Noble, Christina: *Over the High Passes*, Collins, London, 1987.
Randhawa, M. S.: *Travels in the Western Himalayas*, Thomson Press,
    Delhi, 1974.
Scarr, Josephine: *Four Miles High*, Gollancz, London, 1966.
Sharma, M. M.: *Through the Valley of Gods*, Vision Books, New Delhi, 1977.

KISHTWAR
Kolb, Fritz: *Himalayan Venture*, Lutterworth Press, London, 1959.
Venables, S.: *Painted Mountains*, Hodder & Stoughton, London, 1986.

KASHMIR, LADAKH AND ZANSKAR
Cunningham, A.: *Ladakh*, Sagar, New Delhi (reprint 1977), first
    published 1853.
Deacock, Antonia: *No Purdah in Padam*, Harrap, London, 1960.
Gazetteer of Kashmir and Ladakh, Govt. publication, Calcutta, 1890.
Harvey, Andrew: *A Journey in Ladakh*, Jonathan Cape, London, 1983.
Jackson, John A.: *Sonamarg Climbing and Trekking Guide*, Govt of J. & K.,
    Srinagar, 1976.
Mason, Kenneth: *Routes in the Western Himalaya and Kashmir*, G.O.I.
    Press, Calcutta, 1929.
Neve, Dr E. F.: *Beyond Pir Panjal*, Church Missionary Soc., London, 1915.
Noyce, C. W. F.: *A Climber's Guide to Sonamarg*, Himalayan Club,
    New Delhi, 1945.
Peissel, Michel: *Zanskar, the Hidden Kingdom*, Collins and Harvill,
    London, 1979.
Pierre, Bernard: *A Mountain Called Nun Kun*, Hodder & Stoughton,
    London, 1955.
Rizvi, J.: *Ladakh, Cross-road of High Asia*, Oxford University, Delhi, 1983.
Workman, W. H. and F. B.: *Peaks and Glaciers of Nun Kun*, Constable,
    London, 1909.
Younghusband, F.: *Kashmir*, Murray, London, 1909.

EASTERN KARAKORAM
Hillary, Peter: *Rimo*, Hodder & Stoughton, London, 1988.
Khanna, Y. C.: *Saser Kangri*, I.T.B.P., New Delhi, 1980.
Shipton, Eric: *That Untravelled World*, Hodder & Stoughton, London, 1969.
Venables, S.: *Painted Mountains*, Hodder & Stoughton, London, 1986.
Workman, F. and W.: *Two Summers in the Ice-wilds of Eastern
    Karakoram*, T. Fisher Unwin, London, 1912.
Young, Peter: *Himalayan Holiday*, Herbert Jenkins, London, 1943.

INDEX